A PLUME BOOK

WHY WE WRITE

MEREDITH MARAN is the author of ten nonfiction books and the acclaimed 2012 novel *A Theory of Small Earthquakes*. A member of the National Book Critics Circle, she writes features, essays, and book reviews for *People*, *Salon*, the *Ladies' Home Journal*, *Real Simple*, the *Guardian* (London), the *Boston Globe*, the *Chicago Tribune*, and the *San Francisco Chronicle*. She's been a writer in residence at UCLA and at the Mabel Dodge Luhan House, and a fellow at the MacDowell, Mesa Refuge, Ragdale, and Yaddo artists' colonies. Meredith divides her time between sunny writing spots in Oakland and Los Angeles, California.

Why We Write

20 Acclaimed Authors on
How and Why They Do
What They Do

Edited by Meredith Maran

A PLUME BOOK

PLUME
Published by Penguin Group
Penguin Group (USA) Inc., 375 Hudson Street, New York, New York 10014, U.S.A.
Penguin Group (Canada), 90 Eglinton Avenue East, Suite 700, Toronto, Ontario M4P 2Y3,
Canada (a division of Pearson Penguin Canada Inc.) • Penguin Books Ltd, 80 Strand, Lon-
don WC2R 0RL, England • Penguin Ireland, 25 St Stephen's Green, Dublin 2, Ireland (a
division of Penguin Books Ltd) • Penguin Group (Australia), 707 Collins Street, Mel-
bourne, Victoria 3008, Australia (a division of Pearson Australia Group Pty Ltd) • Penguin
Books India Pvt Ltd, 11 Community Centre, Panchsheel Park, New Delhi – 110 017, India
• Penguin Group (NZ), 67 Apollo Drive, Rosedale, Auckland 0632, New Zealand (a division of Pearson New Zealand Ltd) • Penguin Books, Rosebank Office Park, 181 Jan Smuts
Avenue, Parktown North 2193, South Africa • Penguin China, B7 Jaiming Center, 27 East
Third Ring Road North, Chaoyang District, Beijing 100020, China

Penguin Books Ltd., Registered Offices: 80 Strand, London WC2R 0RL, England

First published by Plume, a member of Penguin Group (USA) Inc.

First Printing, February 2013
10 9 8 7 6 5 4 3 2

Copyright © Meredith Maran, 2013
All rights reserved

Each selection is the copyrighted property of its respective author and appears in this volume
by arrangement with the individual writer.

Ⓟ REGISTERED TRADEMARK—MARCA REGISTRADA

LIBRARY OF CONGRESS CATALOGING-IN-PUBLICATION DATA

Maran, Meredith.
  Why we write : 20 acclaimed authors on how and why they do what they do / Meredith
Maran ; with Isabel Allende . . . [et al.].
    p. cm.
  ISBN 978-0-452-29815-6
  1. Authorship. I. Allende, Isabel. II. Title.
  PN165.M37 2013
  810.9'0054--dc23   2012018687

Printed in the United States of America
Set in Adobe Caslon Pro
Designed by Eve L. Kirch

PUBLISHER'S NOTE
While the author has made every effort to provide accurate telephone numbers and Internet
addresses at the time of publication, neither the publisher nor the author assumes any responsibility for errors, or for changes that occur after publication. Further, the publisher does not
have any control over and does not assume any responsibility for author or third-party Web
sites or their content.

For those who read, write, publish, purvey, and love books.

*And in memory of Françoise Sagan, who made me
a reader and a writer and a lover of books.*

Acknowledgments

Becky Cole: Best. Editor. Ever.
Linda Loewenthal: Best. Agent. Ever.

For making magic possible: the MacDowell Colony, Ragdale, the Mesa Refuge, the Virginia Center for the Creative Arts, and Yaddo.

For making this book, and innumerable reading hours, not only possible but delightful: The Twenty.

Contents

Introduction

Why do writers write? Anyone who's ever sworn at a blinking cursor has asked herself that question at some point. Or at many, many points.

When the work is going well, and the author is transported, fingers flying under the watchful eye of the muse, she might wonder, as she takes her first sip of the coffee she poured and forgot about hours ago, "How did I get so lucky, that this is what I get to do?"

And then there are the less rapturous writing days or weeks or decades, when the muse is injured on the job and leaves the author sunk to the armpits in quicksand, and every word she types or scribbles is wrong, wrong, wrong, and she cries out to the heavens, "Why am I doing this to myself?"

It's a curiosity in either case. Why do some people become neurosurgeons, dental hygienists, investment bankers, while others choose an avocation that promises only poverty, rejection, and self-doubt? Why do otherwise rational individuals get up every morning—often very, very early in the morning, before the sun or the family or the day job calls—and willingly enter the cage?

Is it the triumph of seeing one's words in print? Statistics show this isn't a reasonable incentive. According to the website Publishing Explained, more than one million manuscripts are currently searching for a U.S. publisher. One percent of these will get the nod.

Nor can we credit the satisfaction of a job well done. As the ever-cheerful Oscar Wilde put it, "Books are never finished. They are merely abandoned." Only thirty percent of published books turn a profit, so we can rule out material motivation. God knows it can't be for the boost in self-esteem. To paraphrase Charlie Chaplin's depiction of actors, "Writers search for rejection. If they don't get it, they reject themselves."

Why, then, does *anyone* write? Unlike performing brain surgery, cleaning teeth, or trading bonds, *anyone* can pick up a yellow pad or a laptop or a journal and create a poem or a story or a memoir. And, despite the odds against attaining the desired result, many, many people do. We fill our journals and write our novels and take our writing classes. We read voraciously, marveling at the sentences and characters and plot twists our favorite authors bestow upon us. How do they do it? we ask ourselves. And *why?*

"From a very early age, perhaps the age of five or six, I knew that when I grew up I should be a writer. Between the ages of about seventeen and twenty-four I tried to abandon this idea, but I did so with the consciousness that I was outraging my true nature and that sooner or later I should have to settle down and write books."

So declared George Orwell in his 1946 essay "Why I Write," in which he listed the "four great motives for writing":

1. *Sheer egoism.* "To be talked about, to be remembered after death, to get your own back on grown-ups in childhood, etc."

2. *Aesthetic enthusiasm.* "To take pleasure in the impact of one sound on another, in the firmness of good prose or the rhythm of a good story."

3. *Historical impulse.* "The desire to see things as they are, to find out true facts and store them up for the use of posterity."

4. *Political purposes.* "The opinion that art should have nothing to do with politics is itself a political attitude."

Thirty years later Joan Didion reprised the question in *The New York Times Book Review.* "I write entirely to find out what I'm thinking, what I'm looking at, what I see and what it means," Didion wrote. "In many ways writing is the act of saying *I*, of imposing oneself upon other people, of saying *listen to me, see it my way, change your mind.* It's an aggressive, even a hostile act.

"There's no getting around the fact that setting words on paper is the tactic of a secret bully, an invasion, an imposition of the writer's sensibility on the reader's most private space."

In 2001, the preternaturally gentle naturalist Terry Tempest Williams addressed the question in "Why I Write" in *Northern Lights* magazine. "I write to make peace with the things I cannot control. I write to create fabric in a world that often appears black and white. I write to discover. I write to uncover. I write to meet my ghosts. I write to begin a dialogue. I write to imagine things differently and in imagining things differently perhaps the world will change."

As for me: I write books to answer my own questions. So I made a wish list of authors to interview for this one, basing my selections on two factors. I wanted the conversation to benefit from a mix of genres, genders, ethnicities, ages, and, therefore, experiences in writing and in life. And I wanted to talk to those who have beaten the odds: Writers who have succeeded at both the craft and the commerce of writing, who could offer the greatest insights into the creative urge. Writers whose success has satisfied the basic motivations of the struggling author: to become rich and famous, to prove one's work worthy of publication, to prove to one's mother or ex-husband or ex-boss just how wrong that person was. For the household-name authors in this book: done, done, and done.

Those included here—"The Twenty," as I call them— have written books that sell in the kinds of numbers that make publishers send them flowers and leather-bound first editions and, most important, new book contracts. They are authors whose work is regularly praised and sometimes condemned but is rarely ignored by important critics and publications. Their faces and voices are known to anyone who watches *Good Morning America* or listens to *Fresh Air*. Millions or billions of fans worldwide read every book they write.

In other words, the twenty authors here have exactly what every writer wants: full creative freedom and nothing to worry about.

Or so I thought.

*   *   *

I've been publishing poems and articles since Eisenhower was president. I've been writing books and book reviews since Nixon waved good-bye. Decades of assignments have taught me how difficult it can be to elicit a yes from writers as media-wearied as those on my wish list. Publicists, personal assistants, bodyguards, and bouncers have impressed upon me how many requests are rejected daily by those in that stratum of the Famousphere. So I expected the hard part to be the "get": convincing these illustrious few to talk to me.

Q: What might convince the Twenty to sit for interviews for this book?

A: A shared commitment to literacy. And shared support for an organization that promotes it.

826 National fits the bill. It's an innovative youth literacy program, founded in San Francisco in 2002 by the ever-innovative Dave Eggers, now encompassing outposts in Boston; Chicago; Washington, DC; Los Angeles; New York; Seattle; and Ypsilanti, Michigan. Each chapter is housed in a quirkily named storefront (the Boring Store in Chicago; the Museum of Unnatural History in DC) in which after-school tutoring sessions and summer camps are held and from which volunteers fan out into local public schools to help teachers do their jobs—all for free.

Once I'd spoken to the good folks at 826 National and we'd agreed that a portion of the proceeds of this book would go to their worthy projects, I started making calls. The first happy surprise of what proved to be an incredibly happy process: each of the Twenty, from Allende to Wolitzer, said yes. Some said they were eager to support 826. Many said they'd never been asked the "why" question before. They were as interested to answer it as I was to hear their answers.

"Whenever I am writing," Rick Moody told me, "or more accurately, whenever I *have written*, I feel better and more at peace as a human being."

"You have deep control, and where else can you find that?" Meg Wolitzer said. "You can't control other people or your relationships or your children, but in writing you can have sustained periods where you're absolutely in charge."

Sue Grafton said, "My best time as a writer is any day, or any moment, when the work's going well and I'm completely absorbed in the task at hand. The hardest time is when it's not, and I'm not. The latter tend to outnumber the former. But I'm a persistent little cuss. And I soldier on."

Walter Mosley mused, "I can't think of a reason not to write. I guess one reason would be that nobody was buying my books. Come to think of it, that wouldn't stop me. I'd be writing anyway."

I also asked each of the Twenty to share his or her least favorite part of the writing life.

"When I'm working on a book, I'm in a very agitated mental state," Michael Lewis told me. "My sleep is disrupted. I only dream about the project. . . . I'm mentally absent for months at a time. The social cost to my wife and kids is very high. Luckily, I'm a binge writer. I take a lot of time off between books, which is why I still have a family."

"I start all my books on January eighth," Isabel Allende said, shaking her immaculately coiffed head. "Can you imagine January seventh? It's hell . . . I just show up in front of the computer. Show up, show up, show up, and after a while the muse shows up, too."

Pulitzer Prize–winning novelist Jennifer Egan confessed that she worries. A lot. "It was scary, pouring time and energy into a project that didn't have a clear genre identity and might therefore fall through the cracks," she told me. "I'm afraid my publisher will say, 'We can't publish your odd book.' My second-worst fear is that they'll publish it, and the book will come and go without a whisper."

"The only chance in hell I had of being published in the *New Yorker* would have been to sign my cover letters 'J. D. Salinger,'" said David Baldacci.

Most surprising were the writers' responses to the crucial question—a trick question, really—that I'd planted in the mix.

When I asked, "What's the best moment you've had as a writer?" I expected to be regaled with tales of Pulitzers awarded. NEA grants granted. White House readings given. Multiple weeks on bestseller lists. The sort of writerly riches that less-celebrated authors hope to experience someday, should we survive our epic bouts of envy. So I was surprised that so few of the best moments cited by the Twenty had to do with money, fame, or critical recognition.

"Writing my third novel was the best time I've ever had as a writer," Jane Smiley told me, her eyes glowing with the memory. "I felt I was being manipulated from afar. It seemed that the characters were using me as a secretary to write their story."

Nor did Sebastian Junger mention runaway sales or movie deals. "When I went to Sarajevo in '93 and I was with these other freelance writers," he said, "and we were reporting on this incredible story, I went from being a waiter to being a war reporter in the course of three weeks. Seeing your name in print for the first time—nothing can compare to that."

Gish Jen, née Lillian Jen, named her best moment the one when she took her "writing name": "Lillian was a nice Chinese girl," she told me. "Gish was not such a nice girl. Gish was the one propping the doors open so I could get back into the dorm at night. . . . There's a kind of freedom that goes with being Gish that didn't go with being Lillian, and that freedom went with writing."

Each chapter of *Why We Write* revolves around one author's answer to the central question of the book. Each juicy narrative is accompanied by a short excerpt from the author's latest book, a few words of introduction, and a boxed set of stats—"The Vitals" and "The Collected Works"—outlining the author's major milestones, personal and professional.

Why We Write is devoted to the notion that reading is good, and writing is even better. Toward that end, each chapter concludes with the author's pithiest writing tips—a gift to beginning and experienced writers of all genres, genders, ages, ethnicities, and life experiences. The chapters are organized alphabetically based on the authors' last names—one of many reinforcements of the premise of the book: that the status differences among the writers are far less significant than their similarities.

This book is a tribute to writers everywhere, and to the spirit that moves us—as embodied by the Twenty, who gave much of themselves so that 826 National might encourage a few more American kids to love reading and writing, and so that you might find your love of writing and reading enhanced by the book, real or virtual, that you hold in your hands.

Why We Write is an homage, also, to my wonderful agent and my wonderful editor and to all the literary agents, editors, editorial assistants, art directors, book designers, illustrators, copy editors, proofreaders, production managers, compositors, printers, publicists, marketing directors, sales reps, book reviewers, book bloggers, booksellers, and writers of all stripes and polka dots, who continue to adapt to the ever-changing circumstances of their life's work, and who keep one eye in the rearview mirror and one eye on the road ahead, making books so they might reach the people who want, maybe even need, to read them.

Why We Write

CHAPTER ONE

Isabel Allende

In my forty years, I, Zarité Sedella, have had better luck than other slaves. I am going to have a long life and my old age will be a time of contentment because my star—mi z'étoile—also shines when the night is cloudy. I know the pleasure of being with the man my heart has chosen. His large hands awaken my skin.

—Opening lines, *Island Beneath the Sea*, 2010

I sabel Allende is the world's most widely read Spanish-language author. Her name is invariably linked with magical realism, the genre originated by Franz Kafka in the 1920s and popularized by *One Hundred Years of Solitude* author Gabriel García Márquez, to whom Allende is often compared.

But the scope of Allende's work, ranging from historical fiction to bare-all memoirs to the pleasures of food and sex, defies categorization—as does she. A beloved light of the Bay Area literary scene, Allende is first to volunteer when there's a benefit for Hurricane Katrina survivors or a fund-raiser for the public library or when the local indie bookstore needs a boost.

Isabel Allende received me in her cozy, elegantly appointed

Sausalito salon, the front room of the 1907 brothel she bought in 2006. Upstairs her husband, Willie Gordon, practices "people's law." Downstairs, along with her longtime assistant, Juliette Ambatzidis (whose children are counted among Isabel and Willie's grandchildren), Isabel Allende conducts the business end of her avocation: making beautiful words, making a more beautiful world.

THE VITALS

Birthday: August 2, 1942

Born and raised: Born in Lima, Peru; raised in Chile, Bolivia, and Lebanon

Current home: San Rafael, California

Love life: Married 20+ years to attorney Willie Gordon

Family life: "Tribe" includes son Nicolas, grandchildren, family members, and friends

Schooling: Married her first husband at age 20; never attended college

Day job?: No

Honors and awards (partial listing): Feminist of the Year Award, 1994; American Academy of Arts and Letters, 2004; Chilean National Prize for Literature, 2010; 12 international honorary doctorates

Notable notes:

- Isabel Allende's father's first cousin was Salvador Allende, the president of Chile, 1970–73.
- Allende writes in Spanish, and her books are all translated by Margaret Sayers Peden.

- The Isabel Allende Foundation, founded in 1996, "promotes the fundamental rights of women and children to be empowered and protected."
- Allende's 18 books have been translated into 35 languages, with 57 million copies sold.

Website: www.isabelallende.com

Facebook: www.facebook.com/pages/Isabel-Allende/10376 1352995313

Twitter: @isabelallende

THE COLLECTED WORKS

Novels

The House of the Spirits, 1982

The Porcelain Fat Lady, 1984

Of Love and Shadows, 1985

Eva Luna, 1987

The Stories of Eva Luna, 1990

The Infinite Plan, 1991

Daughter of Fortune, 1999

Portrait in Sepia, 2000

City of the Beasts, 2002

Kingdom of the Golden Dragon, 2004

Forest of the Pygmies, 2005

Zorro, 2005

Inés of My Soul, 2006

The Sum of Our Days: A Memoir, 2008

Island Beneath the Sea, 2010

Memoirs

Paula, 1995

Aphrodite: A Memoir of the Senses, 1998

My Invented Country: A Nostalgic Journey Through Chile, 2003

Film Adaptations

The House of the Spirits, 1993

Of Love and Shadows, 1994

Plays

The Ambassador (Chile)

The Ballad of Nobody (Chile)

The Seven Mirrors (Chile)

The House of the Spirits

Paula

Eva Luna (a musical)

Isabel Allende

Why I write

I need to tell a story. It's an obsession. Each story is a seed inside of me that starts to grow and grow, like a tumor, and I have to deal with it sooner or later. Why a particular story? I don't know when I begin. That I learn much later.

Over the years I've discovered that all the stories I've told, all the stories I will ever tell, are connected to me in some way. If I'm talking about a woman in Victorian times who leaves the safety of her home and comes to the Gold Rush in California, I'm really talking about feminism, about liberation, about the process I've gone through in my own life, escaping from a Chilean, Catholic, patriarchal, conservative, Victorian family and going out into the world.

When I start writing a book, I have no idea where it's going. If it's a historical novel I've researched the period and the place, but I don't know what story I want to tell. I only know that in a subtle way or in a hidden way, I want to have an impact on the reader's heart and mind.

I think it might surprise my readers to know how picky I am with language. How I read aloud a paragraph and if there are words repeated, I don't like it. I go through the translation into English line by line. The translator sends me every twenty or thirty pages, and if I see a word that doesn't exactly match my meaning, I go to the dictionary. It's so important for me, finding the precise word that will create a feeling or describe a situation. I'm very picky about that because it's the only material we have: words. But they are free. No matter how many syllables they have: free! You can use as many as you want, forever.

I write in Spanish. I could write a speech in English, but fiction happens in the womb. It doesn't get processed in the mind until you do the editing. But storytelling comes in Spanish to me. It's like making love. I could not be panting in English. It doesn't work that way.

I try to write beautifully, but accessibly. In the romance languages, Spanish, French, Italian, there's a flowery way of saying things that does not exist in English. My husband says he can always tell when he gets a letter in Spanish: the envelope is heavy. In English a letter is a paragraph. You go straight to the point. In Spanish that's impolite.

Reading in English, living in English, has taught me to make language as beautiful as possible, but precise. Excessive adjectives, excessive description—skip it, it's unnecessary. Speaking English has made my writing less cluttered. I try to read *House of the Spirits* now, and I can't. Oh my God, so many adjectives! Why? Just use one good noun instead of three adjectives.

When I tell the story of slavery, I tell it from the slave's point of view. I also go into the master's heart. I want my reader to feel the slave, to understand what it is to not have freedom.

In all my books there are strong women who have to over-come incredible obstacles to have their own destiny. I'm not trying to create models for other women to imitate. I just want my women readers to find the strength. And I want my male readers to understand what it is to be a woman—to find the sympathy.

So I suppose that's it. Then, too, I'm unemployable. What else would I do?

Hell is January seventh

I start all my books on January eighth. Can you imagine January seventh? It's hell.

Every year on January seventh, I prepare my physical space. I clean up everything from my other books. I just leave my dictionaries, and my first editions, and the research materials for the new one. And then on January eighth I walk seventeen steps from the kitchen to the little pool house that is my office. It's like a journey to another world. It's winter, it's raining usually. I go with my umbrella and the dog following me. From those seventeen steps on, I am in another world and I am another person.

I go there scared. And excited. And disappointed—because I have a sort of idea that isn't really an idea. The first two, three, four weeks are wasted. I just show up in front of the computer. Show up, show up, show up, and after a while the muse shows up, too. If she doesn't show up invited, eventually she just shows up.

Heaven is when the muse shows up

When I feel that the story is beginning to pick up rhythm—the characters are shaping up, I can see them, I can hear their voices, and they do things that I haven't planned, things I couldn't have imagined—then I know the book is somewhere, and I just have to find it, and bring it, word by word, into this world.

Then my life changes. Then it becomes a completely different process of excitement, and obsession, and stress. I can work for fourteen hours. Just sitting down for that much time is hard! My son programmed my computer so that every forty-five minutes I have to get up. If I don't, I get so stiff that I can't get up at the end of the day.

I correct to the point of exhaustion, and then finally I say I give up. It's never quite finished, and I suppose it could always be better, but I do the best I can. In time, I've learned to avoid overcorrecting. When I got my first computer and I realized how easy it was to change things ad infinitum, my style became very stiff.

There's a certain charm in what is spontaneous. I want the reader to feel that I'm telling the story to him or her in particular. When you tell a story in the kitchen to a friend, it's full of mistakes and repetitions. I try to avoid that in literature, but I still want it to be a conversation, like storytelling usually is. It's not a lecture.

It's hard to find that balance. But I've been writing for thirty years, so now I know when I'm overdoing it. I read it aloud, and if it's not the way I talk, I change it.

Channeling an eighteenth-century Haitian slave

I have to be very careful with dialogue, because my books are translated into thirty-five languages. It's hard to translate dialogue. Colloquialisms change and the book becomes dated. You never know how your characters' conversations are going to translate to Romanian, to Vietnamese. So I don't use a lot of dialogue. What I do use, I try to keep really simple.

In *Island Beneath the Sea*, the slave couldn't be more different than myself physically or emotionally. She's a tall African woman. Yet I know how I would feel if I was in her place. When I'm writing, I *am* a slave. I *am* on the plantation. I feel the heat, I smell the smells.

Being in the thrall of creating a story, it's a sickness. I carry the story with me all day, all night, in dreams, all the time. Everything I see, everything that happens, it seems to me the universe is talking to me because I connect it to the story. I feel invincible. It could be the most horrible story, but I feel totally happy.

When I was writing my latest book, *Island Beneath the Sea*, I got so awfully sick that I thought I had stomach cancer. I kept vomiting. I couldn't lie down. I had to sleep sitting up. My husband said, "This is your body reacting to the story. When you finish the book, you'll be okay." And that is exactly what happened.

The best time: the first

I've received so many gifts as a writer. I've won awards and prizes. My books have been made into movies and plays. I was even a flag bearer in the 2006 Winter Olympics in Torino, Italy. Can you imagine? I walked into the stadium behind Sophia Loren and before Susan Sarandon. I have a fantastic picture of the ceremony. You see Sophia Loren—beautiful, tall, elegant— and then the flag, and then a hole, and then Susan Sarandon, also beautiful. I'm five feet tall, and I am under the flag. I'm invisible.

But the best time for me was in 1981, when I was writing my first novel. There was no ambition to it, no hope that it would be published, no pressure of any kind. I didn't know yet that I was a writer—I knew that only after I finished my fourth book—so I had no expectations, just the freedom of telling a story for the heck of it.

I worked in my kitchen in Caracas at night, on a little portable typewriter. A typewriter! So I couldn't make mistakes. When I finished the book I showed it to my mother. She said, "Why did you name the worst character in the book after your father?" I never met my father, but I said, "No problem, I'll change the name." So I had to find a name for that character with the same number of letters, and then I had to go through five hundred pages, inserting the new name on each one.

I would cut the pages up with scissors and Scotch tape the corrections in. Some pages had so many corrections, they could stand up and walk.

But the freedom of it! That was a wonderful time, not caring about anything but the story, carrying my one copy of my book everywhere I went, at my breast, like a newborn baby.

The worst time: going dry

My daughter, Paula, died on December 6, 1992. On January 7, 1993, my mother said, "Tomorrow is January eighth. If you don't write, you're going to die."

She gave me the 180 letters I'd written to her while Paula was in a coma, and then she went to Macy's. When my mother came back six hours later, I was in a pool of tears, but I'd written the first pages of *Paula*. Writing is always giving some sort of order to the chaos of life. It organizes life and memory. To this day, the responses of the readers help me to feel my daughter alive.

But after I wrote *Paula*, I went into a writer's block. I would try every day to write, but I was dry inside. After two years of despair, I met Annie Lamott at Book Passage, our local independent bookstore. She asked me if I was doing any better. I said no, I'm worse. She said, "Oh, Isabel, your reservoirs are empty. You have to fill them up." I said, "How can I fill them up?" Annie said, "You'll find a way."

Annie was right. I went with my husband and a friend to India. That shook me up. I asked myself, "Why would I be complaining and whining when there's so much sorrow and wonder in the world? Who am I to be focused only on myself?" That was a wonderful thing.

When I came home, I still couldn't write fiction, so I gave myself a task. I told myself I can write about anything, as long as it's not politics or football.

I needed a subject as removed as possible from the theme of *Paula*. So I wrote *Aphrodite*, a nonfiction book about sex and gluttony.

So now I know that if I'm in a writer's block, I can go back to writing nonfiction. Writing memoirs has its advantages. I know I can never be blackmailed, because I keep no secrets.

But I'm still scared of being unable to write. It's like swallowing sand. It's awful.

Into the future

Storytelling and literature will exist always, but what shape will it take? Will we write novels to be performed? The story will exist, but how, I don't know. The way my stories are told today is by being published in the form of a book. In the future, if that's not the way to tell a story, I'll adapt.

Language: that is what matters to me. Telling a story to create an emotion, a tension, a rhythm—that is what matters to me.

Isabel Allende's Wisdom for Writers

- It's worth the work to find the precise word that will create a feeling or describe a situation. Use a thesaurus, use your imagination, scratch your head until it comes to you, but find the right word.

- When you feel the story is beginning to pick up rhythm—the characters are shaping up, you can see them, you can hear their voices, and they do things that you haven't planned, things you couldn't have imagined—then you know the book is somewhere, and you just have to find it, and bring it, word by word, into this world.

- When you tell a story in the kitchen to a friend, it's full of mistakes and repetitions. It's good to avoid that in literature, but still, a story should feel like a conversation. It's not a lecture.

CHAPTER TWO

David Baldacci

Jack Armstrong sat up in the secondhand hospital bed that had been wedged into a corner of the den in his home in Cleveland. A father at nineteen, he and his wife, Lizzie, had conceived their second child when he'd been home on leave from the army. Jack had been in the military for five years when the war in the Middle East started. . . .

—Opening lines, *One Summer*, 2011

B ased on the theory that adversity builds character—or at least, humility—I didn't expect David Baldacci to possess either trait. He's so good-looking that *People* magazine listed him among its "50 Most Beautiful People in the World." His first book earned him a two-million-dollar advance, became an instant international bestseller, and was made into a movie starring Clint Eastwood. Then there are his book sales: 110 million in print worldwide.

Baldacci did experience adversity along the way. He spent a decade lawyering by day and writing by night—late at night—with nothing to show for his efforts save exhaustion and rejection letters. "The only chance in hell I had of being published in the *New Yorker*," he said, "would have been to sign my cover letters 'J. D. Salinger.'"

David Baldacci is a nice guy. He and his wife run a literacy foundation called Wish You Well. He supports a host of charitable organizations. And he's a nonsectarian president-pleaser. Bill Clinton called *The Simple Truth* his favorite book of 1999. George H. W. Bush signed a note to Baldacci, "Your number one fan in Houston," and invited his favorite author to Kennebunkport for a sit-down.

The Vitals

Birthday: August 5, 1960

Born and raised: Richmond, Virginia

Current home: Vienna, Virginia

Love life: Married 20+ years to Michelle Baldacci

Family life: Two teenaged children (Spencer and Collin); two Labradoodles (Finnegan and Guinness)

Schooling: BA from Virginia Commonwealth University; law degree from University of Virginia

Day job?: No

Honors and awards (partial listing): Gold Medal Award from Southern Writers Guild for best mystery/thriller, 1997; Thumping Good Read Award from W. H. Smith, 1996; People's Choice Award from Library of Virginia, 2005; Silver Bullet Award from International Thriller Writers, 2008; 2011 inductee, International Crime Writing Hall of Fame; 2012 Barnes & Noble Writers for Writers Award

Why We Write*
 15

Notable notes:

- David Baldacci practiced corporate and trial law in Washington, DC, from 1986 to 1995.
- Baldacci is a contributing editor for *Parade* magazine.
- Baldacci's 24 adult novels have been translated into 45 languages, with 110 million copies in print in 80 countries.

Website: www.davidbaldacci.com

Facebook: www.facebook.com/writer.david.baldacci

Twitter: @davidbaldacci

THE COLLECTED WORKS

Novels

Absolute Power, 1996

Total Control, 1997

The Winner, 1997

The Simple Truth, 1998

Saving Faith, 1999

Wish You Well, 2000

Last Man Standing, 2001

The Christmas Train, 2002

Split Second, 2003

Hour Game, 2004

The Camel Club, 2005

The Collectors, 2006

Simple Genius, 2007

Stone Cold, 2007

Divine Justice, 2008

The Whole Truth, 2008

First Family, 2009

True Blue, 2009

Deliver Us from Evil, 2010

Hell's Corner, 2010

One Summer, 2011

The Sixth Man, 2011

Zero Day, 2011

The Innocent, 2012

> **Film Adaptation**
>
> *Absolute Power,* 1997
>
> **Children's Books**
>
> *Freddy and the French Fries: Fries Alive!* 2005
>
> *Freddy and the French Fries: The Mystery of Silas Finklebean,* 2006

David Baldacci

Why I write

If writing were illegal, I'd be in prison. I can't not write. It's a compulsion.

When the sentences and the story are flowing, writing is better than any drug. It doesn't just make you feel good about yourself. It makes you feel good about everything.

It can go the other way, too. When you're deleting page after page, and you just can't make the characters work, and you're running up against deadlines, it's not nearly as euphoric. But actually sitting there and conceiving story ideas and plotting— it's the coolest profession in the world. I'm paid to daydream.

When I was a kid I read a lot. I imagined worlds all the time—little worlds I'd lose myself in. I told my stories to anyone who would listen, and a lot of people who wouldn't. Finally my mom gave me a blank-page notebook. She was trying to shut me up, hoping for a little peace and quiet, and she told me to start writing my stories down. I got hooked.

When you have a bit of imagination and the desire to use words to tell stories, writing takes on a life of its own. When I'm out and about, I can't help but throw the people I see into whatever I'm writing. They have no idea. They'd be scared to death if they knew that I'm walking down the street and they're shooting at me, or I'm shooting at them.

When I go out and talk to schoolkids, I tell them, "All of you are amazingly creative, whether you know it or not. It's adulthood that beats it out of you. If you never lose that, you can go places no one's imagination has ever taken them."

I can't write *Sophie's Choice*. I'm never going to write a book that wins a Pulitzer. I don't think that's what I do, or where my talents lie.

Novels that win prizes like that have great depth. The language, the prose, and the story hold equal power. You can have a sentence that runs for sixteen lines separated by commas. *Sophie's Choice*, for example. That's a thing of beauty.

Could I ever spend five years of my life working on a book, instead of writing a quote-unquote commercial novel in seven, eight, ten months? I don't know if I have the background or the talent to do that. People who write literary fiction are more disciplined. They spend years and years and years and years of their lives on one project. They bring to bear everything they have on that one story.

I spent three years on *Absolute Power* while I was working full-time. It's not a literary novel at all. I tried to develop the characters as much as I could, but it's certainly plot driven. From me, readers want the twists and turns.

AFL versus CIO

This divide between literary and commercial fiction just kills me. It's like splitting a union in half. We have the AFL over here, the CIO over there, and we want you guys to battle against each other because that's going to help . . . oh! Who's that going to help? Big business.

I've gone to book events all over the country, and I've met some terrific literary novelists who welcome commercial writers like me with open arms. It's like, "Hello, comrade!" But I've also seen a lot of animosity. The commercial side complains, "I write books as good as yours, and I never win any prizes." The literary side says, "I write books that are better than yours, and I never sell any books."

Someone once asked John Updike, "Why don't you write a mystery?" And he answered, "Because I'm not smart enough." Here's a guy who's written brilliant fiction, won two Pulitzer Prizes, but he has a different skill set, just as I couldn't have written *Rabbit, Run*. Writing a mystery takes planning and plotting. You lay a bomb on page nine; it doesn't explode till page four hundred. Even a bad book takes some talent and work to put together.

Everyone thinks they can write a novel. They know they can't slam-dunk a basketball because they don't have the height or the athleticism. But people think, "I've got a brain, I've got a laptop. How hard can it be?" Those who attempt it learn that it's very hard to do.

Lawyers are storytellers

Some of the best fiction I ever came up with was as a lawyer.

You know who wins in court? The client whose lawyer tells better stories than the other lawyer does. When you're making a legal case, you can't change the facts. You can only rearrange them to make a story that better enhances your client's position, emphasizing certain things, deemphasizing others. You make sure the facts that you want people to believe are the most compelling ones. The facts that hurt your case are the ones you either explain away or hide away. That's telling a story.

Lawyers work incredibly long hours, and we sell our lives in half-hour increments. Until I finally stopped lawyering in '95, my writing schedule was similar to that. For ten years, I wrote from ten p.m. to two a.m., six nights a week. Draconian, yes, but you find the time where you can. It wasn't hard for me. After a day at work, I had so many stories in my head, I couldn't wait to get home and write them down.

Starving writer: not an option

Growing up in the South, we had some really fine short story writers, like Flannery O'Connor, Truman Capote, Eudora Welty, and Lee Smith. I naturally gravitated toward that form. I started trying to get my short stories published in high school and continued on through college. I collected a lot of rejection letters.

So I bought a book about how to write scripts, and I managed to get an agent, which wasn't easy to do, coming from Virginia. In 1991, while I was billing two hundred dollars an hour as a lawyer, I had a script, and everyone in Hollywood was loving it. My agent said it was going to be a big sale. *Big*. He called me back at midnight and told me that Warner Bros. had passed, which made all the other studios figure there was something wrong with it, so they all passed on it, too.

That was a crushing blow. There had been so much hype,

and I'd believed it. By then I'd been writing a long time. Not that I ever thought I'd make a living as a writer. Even when you got a short story published, the most they'd give you was free copies of the magazine. Not much help for the bank account.

Once our first child was born in 1993, I knew the starving writer route wasn't ever going to work for me. I was the bread-winner, and if I couldn't make any money off the writing, I had to keep making a living as a lawyer. I thought, "It's not going to happen for me. I'll be one of those writers who writes for fun and never gets published." But that didn't mean I was going to stop writing.

I took my best shot

I studied the book industry. I read lots of thrillers and mysteries to see what I was up against. I knew I needed an agent, so I started watching for news stories about first-time novelists sign-ing big book deals. Then I'd go to the bookstore and read that book's acknowledgments page to see who the agent was.

I got seven agents' names that way. I wrote each of them a short query letter: Dear Sir or Madam, I'm a lawyer in DC, I wrote a political thriller, and I guarantee that if you read the first page, you won't stop till you get to the last page. Sincerely, David Baldacci. I thought half of them would read the manu-script just to prove me wrong.

I was hoping to hear back from just one of them, but I heard back from all seven. I went up to New York and met with them. The agent I found is still my agent today.

I did a couple of days' worth of revisions, and then, on a Monday night, my agent sent the manuscript to a bunch of publishers. On Tuesday morning, I was sitting in my law office, and he called me up and said, "Hey, if I sell this manuscript, are you going to be able to quit and write full-time?"

I said, "Well, I've been waiting to do that for the last sixteen years. So yes, that would be very nice." And he said, "Hey, that's good. Because I sold the book."

The chairman of what was then Warner Books had read it overnight and faxed in a preemptive offer: a multimillion-dollar advance for one book. It turned out to be a great deal for the publisher, and a great deal for me as well.

A baby called book

It was surreal. You have to realize that nobody except my wife, my parents, my brother, and my sister knew I'd been writing all those years. My wife and I called our friends and said, "We have something special to tell you." They thought we were having another baby. I said, "Actually, we are having another baby. But I'm the one delivering it. It's called a book."

All I'd known to that point was rejection, so for the next year I kept my day job. Finally my wife and I sat down and I said, "This is something I've been working for my whole life. I'd like to have my shot." We agreed I'd quit, and if the book flopped I'd go back to practicing law. It was nerve-wracking, waiting for the book to come out. I knew if it didn't sell, with a big advance like that, I was done.

This sounds a little corny, but the day I felt I'd made it as a writer was the first time I saw a book of mine on a bookstore shelf—in the Borders in the World Trade Center. After that I stopped waiting for the publishers to say, "We've had a change of plans. You have to give the money back." I realized the writing career was working out.

Scared to death. Every time.

Every time I start a project, I sit down scared to death that I won't be able to bring the magic again.

You'd never want to be on the operating table with a right-handed surgeon who says, "Today I'm going to try operating with my left hand." But writing is like that. The way you get better is by pushing yourself to do things differently each time. As a writer you're not constrained by mechanical devices or technology or anything else. You get to play. Which is terrifying.

William Goldman, who wrote the script for *Absolute Power*, gave me some great advice. He said, "Write everything as if it's the first thing you ever wrote. The day you think you know how to do it is the day you're done as a writer." He was right. If writing ever becomes a job for me—if I start thinking I'd rather be out playing tennis, so I start taking shortcuts, doing it this time the same way I did it last time—I'll hang it up.

Sometimes I envy myself twenty years ago, sitting in my little cubbyhole with nobody knocking on my door, writing stories without worrying about the touring, the money, the foreign travel. But every day I try to face the screen as if there's no commercial world out there, as if I'm doing it for free, for the pure joy of telling my stories, the way I did it for the first sixteen years.

David Baldacci's Wisdom for Writers

- Whatever genre you write in, familiarize yourself with what's current in your genre. What thrilled the reader even ten years ago doesn't necessarily thrill today. Check out the competition.

- Whether you're writing a novel or a cover letter to a potential agent, shorter is always better. Remember what Abraham Lincoln said, paraphrasing Pascal: "I'm sorry I wrote such a long letter. I did not have time to write a short one."

- The upside of the current state of publishing: it's a lot easier to self-publish than it ever was. Publish on the Internet, or on demand, or self-publish in print—but whatever you do, if you want to share your story, *publish it.*

- "Writing for your readers" is a euphemism for "writing what you think people will buy." Don't fall for it! Write for the person you know best: yourself.

CHAPTER THREE

Jennifer Egan

It began the usual way, in the bathroom of the Lassimo Hotel. Sasha was adjusting her yellow eye shadow in the mirror when she noticed a bag on the floor beside the sink that must have belonged to the woman whose peeing she could faintly hear through the vaultlike door of a toilet stall. . . .

—Opening lines, *A Visit from the Goon Squad*, 2010

How is Jennifer Egan exceptional? Reviewing her 2006 novel, *The Keep*, the *New York Times* counted the ways. "Jennifer Egan is a refreshingly unclassifiable novelist; she deploys most of the arsenal developed by metafiction writers of the 1960s and refined by more recent authors like William T. Vollmann and David Foster Wallace—but she can't exactly be counted as one of them. The opening of her novel *The Keep* lays out a whole Escherian architecture, replete with metafictional trapdoors, pitfalls, infinitely receding reflections, and trompe l'oeil effects, but what's more immediately striking about this book is its unusually vivid and convincing realism."

But it's not just the way Egan writes that makes her one of a kind; it's *what* she writes. Journalism in the *New York Times*

Magazine, among other venues. Short stories. Book reviews. Novels, each one dramatically different from the last—most notably *A Visit from the Goon Squad*, the book she refuses to classify. "It was scary, pouring time and energy into a project that didn't have a clear genre identity and might therefore fall through the cracks," Egan told me in a 2010 interview for *Salon*. "The economy had crashed since I'd published my last novel. I thought my publisher might say, 'This isn't the moment to publish an odd book.' Or that even if I sold the novel, it might come and go without a whisper."

It was that brave, odd book that won Jennifer Egan the Pulitzer Prize for fiction.

THE VITALS

Birthday: September 6, 1962

Born and raised: Born in Chicago, Ilinois; raised in San Francisco, California

Current home: Fort Greene, Brooklyn

Love life: Married to director David Herskovits

Family life: Two sons, ages 9 and 11

Schooling: University of Pennsylvania; University of Cambridge, England

Day job?: No

Honors and awards (partial listing): National Endowment for the Arts Fellowship; Guggenheim Fellowship; Fellow at the New York Public Library; finalist for PEN/Faulkner Award for fiction; National Book Critics Circle Award for fiction; Pulitzer Prize for fiction; LA Times Book Prize

Notable notes:

• Jennifer Egan grew up in San Francisco, where she graduated from Lowell, the city's most academically competitive
public high school.
• Explaining why she included a PowerPoint presentation as
a chapter in *A Visit from the Goon Squad*, and why she
doesn't classify the book as either a novel or a short story
collection, Egan said, "My ground rules were: every piece
has to be very different . . . I actually tried to break that
rule later; if you make a rule then you should also break it!"

Website: www.jenniferegan.com

Facebook: www.facebook.com/jennifereganwriter?ref=sgm

Twitter: @egangoonsquad

THE COLLECTED WORKS

Novels

The Invisible Circus, 1995

Look at Me, 2001

The Keep, 2006

A Visit from the Goon Squad, 2010

Film Adaptations

The Invisible Circus, 1999

The Keep (in production)

Fiction Collection

Emerald City, short
stories, 1996

Jennifer Egan

Why I write

When I'm not writing I feel an awareness that something's missing. If I go a long time, it becomes worse. I become depressed. There's something vital that's not happening. A certain slow damage starts to occur. I can coast along awhile without it, but then my limbs go numb. Something bad is happening to me, and I know it. The longer I wait, the harder it is to start again.

When I'm writing, especially if it's going well, I'm living in two different dimensions: this life I'm living now, which I enjoy very much, and this completely other world I'm inhabiting that no one else knows about. I don't think my husband can tell. It's a double life I get to live without destroying my marriage. And it's heaven.

Especially when I'm writing a first draft, I feel as if I've been transported out of myself. That's always a state I'm trying to achieve, even as a journalist—although when I'm working on nonfiction I'm almost never actually writing. I do months of research and then write the piece in a few days.

When I'm writing fiction I forget who I am and what I come from. I slip into utter absorption mode. I love the sense that I've become so engaged with the other side, I've slightly lost my bearings here. If I'm going from the writing mind-set to picking my kids up from school, I often feel a very short but acute kind of depression, as if I have the bends. Once I'm with them it totally disappears, and I feel happy again. Sometimes I forget I have children, which is very strange. I feel guilty about it, as if my inattention will cause something to happen to them, even when I'm not responsible for them—that God will punish me.

When the writing's going well—I'm trying not to sound clichéd—I feel fueled by a hidden source. During those times it doesn't matter if things are going wrong in my life; I have this alternate energy source that's active. When the writing's going poorly, it's as bad or worse than not writing at all. There's a leak or a drain, and energy is pouring out of it. Even when the rest of my life is fine, I feel like something's really bad. I have very little tolerance for anything going wrong, and I take little joy from the good things. It was worse before I had kids. I appreciate that they make me forget what's going on professionally.

Anticipation trumps reality

This is an interesting moment to consider why I write, because I'm not writing now. When I'm where I am now, and I haven't yet started the next book, boy, is that next book going to be great! It's lots easier to think that than when you're actually writing it. Fantasy provides its own satisfactions.

I can't begin a new novel while I'm working on anything else. I'm desperate for traction with fiction, and I can't get it till I put pen to paper. Now I've got my sights set on the New Year. Before that it was September. Before that it was summer. It's definitely time to get involved in a large project. I feel that keenly. All I ever have to begin with is the when and where of a novel. I have a good feeling about those elements of my next one, but in the end, when and where is not a book.

The girl with the throwaway novel

My first attempt at writing a novel was horrible. I had to throw it away. But I stuck with the idea, which is what became *The Invisible Circus*.

When I was twenty-nine I got an NEA grant, which gave me a year to work on *Circus*. I finished the first draft and sat down to read it, hoping I'd find it to be fantastic. Instead I read it and found it to be really weak. I didn't get far in my reading; I went crazy before I could even get to the middle. How far it seemed from something you could sell or want to read was really scary.

I went into this three-day panic attack that was quite extreme. This was before I'd ever had therapy. I was pushing thirty. I'd quit my job as a private secretary when I got the grant. And now the NEA money was running out. I had to find another job, and I had no professional track record except as a temp.

All those worries flared into a mania when I read the draft. I really went haywire. I was walking around the East Village having the worst panic attack I've ever had. It was harrowing. I was calling people, apologizing for saying I'd ever be a writer. I felt very unstable, like my whole life had no point. It was a genuine existential crisis. I didn't eat for four days. I was like a gaunt specter of terror lurking around the East Village in a trench coat. I'd just started living with the man who became my husband. He'd come home from rehearsal, and I'd pounce on him, needing to be resuscitated. I imagined him thinking, "Oh, God, what have I gotten myself into? This girl is out of her mind."

Somehow I managed to get out of this nutty behavior. In four days I was back at work on the novel. I tore the thing apart and put it back together. Amid all that hand-wringing, and moping and weeping, some other part of my brain was thinking about how I could improve the manuscript. It wasn't long before I wanted to enact those improvements. And once I was back in it, making it better, I immediately calmed down. All that wheel-spinning, all that agony resulted in a clear logistical plan.

That's how it seems to work for me. I can be wigging out, but I'm also working.

Look at me: cross-eyed

Working on *Look at Me* was the most painful experience I've had as a writer. It was a huge struggle. I'm not quite sure why I suffered to the degree I did, working on that book, but I do know that my work up to that point had been fairly conventional, and I didn't know if anyone would accept that kind of book from me. It was almost as if I thought I'd be punished for it. I felt afraid as I worked on it. I thought it was terrible, that I was reaching too far.

At the same time, some of the most exciting moments I've had as a writer were during the writing of that book, even with all those worries and that feeling of doom. One day I read the first six chapters of the book in one sitting, and I tore out of the house and went running, and I had this sense that I'd never read anything quite like that before, that I'd done something really different. That was such a thrilling feeling.

On the other hand, writing *The Keep* and *Goon Squad* were

only difficult until I'd arrived at a voice for each of them. From then on, they were sheer fun. Once I got the voice I was in heaven. *The Keep*, especially, was a romp.

It's all about seeing what's wrong

One of my strengths as a writer is that I'm a good problem solver. I write these unthinking, ungoverned first drafts. The project for me always is to turn that instinctive stuff into pages that work.

I want all the flights of fancy, and I can only get them in a thoughtless way. So I allow myself that. Which means that my next step has to be all about problem solving. My attitude cannot be, Gee, I wrote it, it's good. I'd never get anywhere. It's all about seeing what's wrong from a very analytical place. It's a dialectic.

Once I have a draft I make the plans, edit on hard copy, and make an extensive outline for the revision. The revision notes I wrote for *Look at Me* were eighty pages long.

Winning the Pulitzer: priceless

The response to *Goon Squad* has definitely made me a happier person. There's a deep joy and satisfaction in getting external acknowledgment of that magnitude. Winning the Pulitzer, specifically, feels like a thousand wishes being granted. All these years I've had a longing for some kind of massive approval—not thinking I deserved it, but just wanting it. I never thought it would happen.

This is a big change. I don't think it's changing me, but it's a change I feel on a daily, hourly basis in a very positive way. If you can't enjoy this, my God, it's really time to go back into therapy. It's delicious!

In one hundred years, if humans still exist, and if anyone remembers the name Jennifer Egan, they'll decide whether I deserve the Pulitzer or not. The question doesn't preoccupy me. I've judged a major prize and I know how it works. It all comes down to taste, and therefore, luck. If you happen to be in the final few, it's because you're lucky enough to have written something that appeals to those particular judges' tastes.

I think my book is strong, and I know I did a good job. I also know it could have been better. There are plenty of books out there that are also good, and those writers could also have had the luck I had. Deserving only gets you so far. Winning a prize like that has a lot to do with cultural forces; with appetites at work in the culture.

Honestly, I prefer *Look at Me*. Maybe I'm just being stubborn because *Goon Squad* gets so much love, but *Look at Me* is the one that's stayed with me imaginatively. *Goon Squad* may have ended up being more ambitious than I thought it would be, but for whatever reason, *Look at Me* dug into me. That doesn't mean it's better. It probably has more flaws than *Goon Squad*. But *Look at Me* is my favorite child.

Winning the Pulitzer: dangerous

The attention and approval I've been getting for *Goon Squad*—the very public moments of winning the Pulitzer and the other prizes—is exactly the opposite of the very private pleasure of writing. And it's dangerous. Thinking that I'll get this kind of love again, that getting it should be my goal, would lead me to creative decisions that would undermine me and my work. I've never sought that approval, which is all the more reason that I don't want to start now.

I'm curious to find out what influence this will have on my writing. I won't know until I start another book. A scenario I could easily envision is the following: I start the book, feel it's not going well, and start to freak. My rational side says, "Let's get one thing straight. You're going to hate the next one. The whole world's going to hate the next one." I have no idea why this one got so much love.

But part of me thinks, They liked my last book. Hurray. Now we move on. That moving on will undoubtedly involve massive disappointment on the part of others. It never happens this way twice. In a way, I find that sort of freeing. My whole creative endeavor is the repudiation of my last work with the new one. If I start craving approval, trying to replicate what I did with *Goon Squad*, it's never going to lead to anything good. I know that. Stop getting better? There's no excuse for that.

I hope I can just start the next novel, engage in that alternate world, enjoy myself, and accept and internalize the expectation that the book will not be perceived as being as good as *Goon Squad*, and who cares. It's lucky to have a book the world loves this much. Most people never have that experience.

We all have such a tendency to think the present moment will last forever. Maybe when I'm not the flavor of the month anymore I'll be devastated and shocked, and I'll forget everything I'm saying this minute. But my hope is that I have the tools to handle it.

Jennifer Egan's Wisdom for Writers

- Read at the level at which you want to write. Reading is the nourishment that feeds the kind of writing you want to do. If what you really love to read is y, it might be hard for you to write x.

- Exercising is a good analogy for writing. If you're not used to exercising you want to avoid it forever. If you're used to it, it feels uncomfortable and strange not to. No matter where you are in your writing career, the same is true for writing. Even fifteen minutes a day will keep you in the habit.

- You can only write regularly if you're willing to write badly. You can't write regularly and well. One should accept bad writing as a way of priming the pump, a warm-up exercise that allows you to write well.

Chapter Four

James Frey

First time I saw him he was coming down the hallway. There
was an apartment across the hall from where I lived that'd
been empty for a year. Usually apartments in our project go
quick. Government supports them so they're cheap, for people
who ain't got shit in this world and, even though they always
telling us different, know we ain't ever gonna have shit.

—Opening lines, *The Final Testament of the Holy Bible*, 2011

In January 2006, the world—or at least, Oprah Winfrey's world—watched as Oprah chastised James Frey, the author of *A Million Little Pieces*, her famous book club's most recent pick. Oprah accused Frey of having misrepresented himself and several events in the book.

"Did you cling to that image because that's how you wanted to see yourself?" Oprah asked Frey. "Or did you cling to that image because that would make a better book?"

"Probably both," Frey replied.

"I feel really duped," Oprah concluded. "I feel that you betrayed millions of readers."

The Frey debacle hit the pause button on the memoir genre,

putting many memoirists out of work. Those lucky enough to find publishers were obliged to write what became known as "a Frey disclaimer," in hopes of avoiding the lawsuits that Frey's book spawned—one of which forced his publisher to offer a refund to those who had bought a copy.

The investigation continued; new facts emerged. It turned out that Frey had initially shopped his book as a work of fiction. His publisher, seeking greater sales, had positioned it as a true story. Frey had proposed a disclaimer explaining the difference; his request was denied. But 2006 was an American moment rife with deception and outrage. Think Iraq War. Think "weapons of mass destruction." Think Stephen Colbert's new noun, "truthiness." As *New York Times* columnist Maureen Dowd wrote, following Frey's 2006 *Oprah* appearance, "It was a huge relief, after our long national slide into untruth and no consequences, into swiftboating and swift bucks, into W's delusion and denial, to see the Empress of Empathy icily hold someone accountable for lying."

Five years later, during *Oprah*'s final season, she invited James Frey onto her show again—twice. "Most writers of memoirs do what I did," Frey said. "I apologize for my lack of compassion," Oprah replied. And then the two of them hugged and made up.

Meet James Frey. Judge for yourself. Or better yet, learn from his experience what you can, and don't judge him at all.

THE VITALS

Birthday: September 12, 1969

Born and raised: Cleveland, Ohio

Current home: New York, New York

Love life: Married, with three children

Schooling: Denison University; Art Institute of Chicago

Day job?: Founder of Full Fathom Five, 2010

Notable notes:

- James Frey lists among his previous occupations: playing Santa Claus and the Easter Bunny in a department store, stock boy, doorman, janitor, screenwriter, director, and producer.
- *A Million Little Pieces* was rejected by 17 publishers before Doubleday agreed to publish it. The book has since sold more than 7 million copies worldwide, in 35 languages.
- The sequel, *My Friend Leonard*, was also a *New York Times* bestseller.
- The book that influenced Frey most is *Tropic of Cancer* by Henry Miller.

Website: www.bigjimindustries.com

Facebook: www.facebook.com/profile.php?id=547390762

THE COLLECTED WORKS

Memoirs

A Million Little Pieces, 2003

My Friend Leonard, 2005

Novels

Bright Shiny Morning, 2008

The Final Testament of the Holy Bible, 2011

Essays and Illustrated Books

American Pitbull, 2008

Wives, Wheels, Weapons (photo-illustrated by Terry Richardson), 2008

Screenplays

Kissing a Fool, 1998

Sugar, 1998

I Am Number Four, 2011

James Frey

Why I write

I'm really not qualified to do anything else. At this point it's so much a part of my life that I can't not do it. If I don't work I go crazy. And frankly, I have a family, and I need the money.

When I was a little boy I loved to get lost in books. I never thought about becoming a writer until I was twenty-one and I read *Tropic of Cancer*. Very few things in my life have spoken to me the way that book did. I had never encountered something that spoke to me so purely and so directly and so profoundly. Half of it was rage and half of it was joy, and it was exactly how I felt about the world.

The only other place I'd seen an articulation so beautiful and so bold was in a Jackson Pollock painting. Those paintings speak to me the same way because they're made by an artist who said, "I don't give a fuck, this is what I do, this is how I'm going to do it, this is what it is. You can love it or hate it. This is not about you."

I was like, That's what I'm going to do. And six months later I moved to Paris because *Tropic of Cancer* was about Henry Miller living there. Moving to Paris was about searching and looking and living and trying to become a writer and trying to figure out what that meant, if it was even possible. To live boldly, recklessly, stupidly, and beautifully.

The historical impulse

I try to write books I wish other people had written, books I wish I'd read. People always say I'm arrogant when I talk about this, but I think I'm one of the few people who's honest about what Orwell called "the historical impulse." I want to write historically important books, books that matter, books that change the world, that change writing and change publishing.

I look over the course of literary history, and I think, yeah, I can place myself—I have the potential to place myself—among these people: the writers I love, the writers who have made history. I want to place myself within the canon.

Certainly a lot of it is ego. To say it's not is bullshit. I'm competitive about it. I'm sitting at my desk right now, and the only picture on my wall, other than drawings made by my children, is a *Sports Illustrated* cover of Marvelous Marvin Hagler, who was the middleweight boxing champ through the 1980s. The headline is "The Best and the Baddest." That speaks to me. I want to be the best and the baddest.

Earlier in my career it was about making the mark. Now it's about trying to deepen the mark and make it permanent. I said it in the first interview I ever gave years ago. I want to be the most widely read, most controversial, most influential writer of my time.

Getting lost

The thing I love most about the act of writing is that I disappear. I get lost in trying to make every word the right word, in trying to tell the story.

When I'm writing I have total control. Nothing's going on the page unless I put it there. It's not going to stay there unless I want it to stay there. When you sit down at the machine, you create that world, you live in that world, you control that world, it's only whatever you want it to be. There's no time when I'm more content, more at ease, than when it's just me alone in a room for eight hours.

It took me years to get to that place where I sit down and I know I'm going to write the way I want to write, and it's going to be good. I don't write normally. I don't use standard grammar or punctuation. I don't do anything right. That's all deliberate, but it took me a long time to find the confidence to violate every rule that exists.

A lot of the games writers play with themselves, especially young writers, are games of confidence. "Can I do this? Oh, it's so hard, it's not coming out the way I want it to come out." A lot of writers get lost trying to find their way. A lot of writers never find it.

When I sit down at the machine there's no doubt for me.

When I'm away from it, thinking about it, I have great fears. But when I'm at the computer I always believe I can do what I want to do. It might take me a long time, it might be hard, it might be lonely. But I always believe the book I'm starting is going to be what I want it to be. Why? Because I fucking control it. Once you have that in your life you can't let it go, ever.

I work a lot in the movies and in TV, and that's one of the frustrations. You have to have a totally different mind-set, because you're not in control anymore.

Getting found

After I read *Tropic of Cancer* I kept trying to find a way to write that made sense to me. I couldn't do it. I kept writing all kinds of crap. Garbage.

Then I sat down and I wrote the first thirty pages of *A Million Little Pieces* in one sitting. It took me about four hours. I've never written that fast before or since. After I had that short burst I sat back and looked at what I'd written and I was like, yup, yup.

On the first page of *Tropic of Cancer*, Miller says, "I no longer think I am an artist. I am one." I saw those thirty pages and I was like, There it is, man, there it is.

Rich beats poor

I'd been poor, and it sucked, and I didn't want a shit job in a bar or a clothing store. So I started writing movies when I was twenty-five. The end game was always writing books, but there were plenty of dudes making dough writing bad movies. I thought, I can do that.

I wrote the corniest, most commercial romantic comedy I could, in a pure, mercenary way, and I moved from Chicago to Los Angeles and I sold it. Between twenty-five and thirty-one I was a journeyman screenwriter. I had a job as a writer, but that's different from being a writer.

After I wrote that little burst of *A Million Little Pieces*, I knew I could do what I wanted to do. I just needed time. I took a second mortgage on my house. I had enough money for eighteen months. It took me about a year to write *A Million Little Pieces*, and then I sold it. And that's what I've been doing since.

I still do movies. I had a movie come out in 2011, a big, corny, DreamWorks teenage action movie called *I Am Number Four* that I did under a fake name.

Persona of interest

It's funny to me to use fake names. Being a writer is about creating public mythology, creating a writerly persona, as much as it's about what you write.

There's James Frey who goes home to his family, and there's the public James Frey. Look at guys like Hemingway or Kerouac or Bukowski or Norman Mailer or Hunter Thompson. I'm willing to bet the person who was home with his family wasn't the guy the public thought of as that person. These people had big public personas, and their public personas almost destroyed them. They got lost. They forgot that there's a line between who you are at home and who you are in public.

At this point in my career there's the public James Frey: bad

James Frey, notorious James Frey, egomaniac, arrogant James Frey. Who I am at home is different. I don't need to swagger into my apartment and say I'm the best and the baddest. When I go home I'm just Daddy. I'm James, my wife's husband.

In my personal life there are plenty of things I'm insecure about. I'm scared I'll wake up someday and not have money to pay my bills. I get nervous at parties; I don't like being around forty people at once. Pretty standard human bullshit.

I've had shitty things happen to me in my career—like getting eviscerated by Oprah on national TV, and having sixteen class-action lawsuits filed against me, and having a lawyer tell me, "You're facing permanent financial Armageddon. You should think about moving to Florida or Switzerland or Monaco."

But what scares me most is that something might happen to my kids. My wife and I had a second child who passed away. A son. That's the most brutal experience ever.

Compared to losing a kid, losing a friend, having your heart broken—those horrific experiences as a writer are just bad days at work. Two thousand six was a bad year at work for me, but that's all it was.

When I'm at the machine, when I'm James Frey the writer, all that evaporates. I have no doubt. I have no fear. Nobody can hurt me, nobody can say shit that means anything to me. When I'm in the act of writing it's not ego, it's just work, just struggle and challenge. I keep a pretty strict wall between those things. People get into trouble when that wall falls down.

My writing, me, all of it, is a big, long-running piece of performance art. The die has been cast. The mythology exists. Whether it lasts or not will be determined by how good the books I write are. That's the beauty of it: all the bullshit in the world, and all that really matters to me, to readers, to history, is, Are the books good enough? What I want is to do to other people what Henry Miller did to me.

Radical

As I was trying to teach myself to write the way I wanted to, I looked a lot at literary history. I tried to figure out what different writers I admired had in common with one another.

I looked at people like Baudelaire, Fitzgerald, Henry Miller, John Dos Passos, Hemingway, Kerouac, Mailer, Thompson, Ginsberg, Bret Easton Ellis. When their writing first appeared nobody had seen anything like it. Take *On the Road*. How many road books existed before that? Billions. *Don Quixote* is a road book, two guys going on a trip. You have to radically reinvent not just how writing can be done, but how subject matter can be treated. You have to write great books, singular books that are absolutely unique and almost revolutionary and immediately identifiable as yours.

We think of Hemingway now and it's just Hemingway. But when his books first came out—short, declarative sentences, tight, lean, easy to read, plot-intensive writing—it was radical. If you think about Kerouac, radical. Henry Miller, radical. Ginsberg, radical.

The best best of all

I've had some spectacular moments as a writer. It's awesome the first time you see your book in a bookstore; the first time somebody says, "Damn, dude, I love your books." I love starting a book and finishing a book. There's pure pleasure when you feel like you wrote a sentence that's perfect for whatever it needs to be. I've had readings with thousands of people at them, I've sold ten or fifteen million books, I get to go on book tours around the world. At one point I was number one on both the hardcover and paperback *New York Times* bestseller lists.

You would think that would be the greatest moment. But it wasn't.

The greatest moment—I might even start crying when I talk about it—was when I typed the last word of *A Million Little Pieces*. I looked at it and burst out into tears. I don't know if there will ever be a moment in my writing career better than that.

I have a deal with myself. If I'm ever more concerned with what people are saying or with what my sales are or how many people show up at my readings than I am with writing shit that rocks people's worlds, I'll quit and find something else to do. I'm not going to be some seventy-five-year-old man who's just cranking shit out because my ego won't let it go.

Marvin Hagler just walked away from boxing one day. Everyone was asking, "When's he coming back?" He's never coming back. I have huge respect for the way he did that.

At some point I'll just leave, and nobody will ever hear from me again.

James Frey's Wisdom for Writers

- In true art there are no rules. It doesn't have to be fiction or nonfiction. You don't have to have gone to a certain school or have an MFA. Either you can write or you can't.

- Work hard.

- Thanks to e-books, publishers aren't necessary anymore. If you want to publish a book, do it yourself.

- Believe in yourself. If I can do it, you can do it.

CHAPTER FIVE

Sue Grafton

Phillip Lanahan drove to Vegas in his 1985 Porsche 911
Carrera Cabriolet, a snappy little red car his parents had
given him two months before, when he graduated from
Princeton. His stepfather bought the car secondhand because he
abhorred the notion of depreciation. Better that the original
owner take that hit.

—Opening lines, *V Is for Vengeance*, 2011

I dare you: read a page one like the one above and put the book down. Go ahead and try.

"Bet you can't read just one" could be Sue Grafton's brand identity. And—in addition to being a gifted writer who rightly prides herself on her rare dual achievements, rave reviews *and* blockbuster sales—Grafton *is* a brand. Fortunately for her millions of readers in twenty-eight countries and twenty-six languages, she's a brand with twenty-five built-in sequels.

Published in 1982, when Grafton was a forty-two-year-old successful but unhappy screenwriter, *A Is for Alibi* was the first in her mystery series featuring female private investigator Kinsey Millhone. *A* wasn't, in fact, Grafton's first novel. She wrote her first at age eighteen, and six more in quick succession, only two of which, *Keziah Dane* (1967) and *The Lolly-Madonna War* (1969), were published. After years at author boot camp, a.k.a. screenwriting, an irresistible mystery plot presented itself. Enmeshed in bitter divorce proceedings, Grafton found herself fantasizing about murdering or, at least, maiming, her soon-to-be ex-husband. Luckily for all of us, she turned those fantasies into a novel. Grafton has already completed *A* through *V* in the series. Never have so many wished so fervently to add a few more letters to the alphabet.

THE VITALS

Birthday: April 24, 1940

Born and raised: Louisville, Kentucky

Current home: Montecito, California, and Louisville, Kentucky

Love life: Married 33 years to science lecturer Dr. Steven F. Humphrey

Family life: Three adult children, four granddaughters (including one named Kinsey)

Schooling: Graduated from the University of Louisville, 1961, with a BA in English literature

Day job?: No

Honors and awards (partial listing): Three Anthony Awards, three Shamus Awards, the Smith-Breckenridge Distinguished Woman of Achievement Award, the Ross Macdonald Literary Award, the Diamond Dagger Lifetime Achievement Award from the British Crime Writers' Association, a Grand Master Award from Mystery Writers of America

Notable notes:

- Sue Grafton is the daughter of detective novelist C. W. Grafton.
- Grafton cites Ross Macdonald as her strongest literary influence. She set her "alphabet series" in the fictional town of Santa Teresa, California, which Macdonald had created as a stand-in for Santa Barbara.
- It wasn't until *G Is for Gumshoe* that Grafton earned enough money as a writer to quit her day job.
- Grafton has refused to sell film rights to her books and has threatened to haunt her children if they do so after her death.

Website: www.suegrafton.com

Facebook: www.facebook.com/pages/sue-grafton/1125660 22091435?ref=ts

THE COLLECTED WORKS

Novels

Keziah Dane, 1967

The Lolly-Madonna War, 1969

A Is for Alibi, 1982

B Is for Burglar, 1985

C Is for Corpse, 1986

D Is for Deadbeat, 1987

E Is for Evidence, 1988

F Is for Fugitive, 1989

G Is for Gumshoe, 1990

H Is for Homicide, 1991

I Is for Innocent, 1992

J Is for Judgment, 1993

K Is for Killer, 1994

L Is for Lawless, 1995

M Is for Malice, 1996

N Is for Noose, 1998

O Is for Outlaw, 1999

Sue Grafton

Why I write

I write because in 1962 I put in my application for a job working in the children's department at Sears, and they never called me back.

Seriously: I write because it's all I know how to do. Writing is my anchor and my purpose. My life is informed by writing, whether the work is going well or I'm stuck in the hell of writer's block, which I'm happy to report only occurs about once a day.

My best time as a writer is any day, or any moment, when the work's going well and I'm completely absorbed in the task at hand. The hardest time is when it's not, and I'm not. The latter tend to outnumber the former. But I'm a persistent little cuss. And I soldier on.

I'm a persistent writer. And also a terrified one.

Most days when I sit down at my computer, I'm scared half out of my mind. I'm always convinced that my last book was my last book, that my career is at an end, that I'll never be able to pull off another novel, that my success was a fleeting illusion, and my hopes for the future are already dead. Dang! All this drama and it's not even nine a.m.

Writer's block is a subject I've given a lot of thought to, since I come up against it so often. I used to try to power through, overriding the block by sheer force of will. Now I look at it differently. I see writer's block as a message from Shadow, informing me that I'm off track. The "block" is the by-product of a faulty choice I've made. My job is to back up and see if I can pinpoint the fork in the road where I headed in the wrong direction. Sometimes I've misunderstood a character or his or her motivation. Sometimes I've laid out events in a sequence that muddies the story line. Usually I don't have to retrace my steps more than a chapter or two, and the error is easily corrected.

I write largely by trial and error, which means I often run into dead ends. I pursue possibilities that peter out. I devise and abandon whole story lines because they turn out to be unusable.

To steady myself, I keep a series of journals for every novel I write. That's where I allow myself to whine, wring my hands, fret, scheme, experiment, and occasionally pat myself on the back. Writing is tense and stressful work. My theory is that if I don't own my dark side—my frustration, my fears, and the bumbling about I seem destined to do on any given day—my negative emotions will sabotage my ability to write.

My working journals serve several purposes. They give me

a record of my process, a day-by-day account of the problems I see as a book takes shape. When I come up against writer's block, I go back and read the journals from the early stages of the writing. As odd as this sounds, more than once I've solved a problem and tagged the solution long before I began the actual writing.

Another joy of keeping journals is that on days when I'm feeling especially frustrated and despairing, I can read through the journals from an earlier book and realize that I felt just as baffled and frightened when I was writing that one. Knowing that I've survived all my bumbling and fumbling in the past helps me survive it in the present. And sometimes, the odd and unrelated ideas that occur to me while I'm writing one book spark an idea for the next book in the series. I don't know if other writers operate this way, but it's worked for me.

When I reread the journals, I can see I'm telling myself the story in endless loops, repeating myself until I can see the whole of a narrative. So the journals are incredibly boring. I don't try to be literate or lofty, and I ignore the fact that one day someone else might read every tedious page. The purpose of the journals isn't to impress myself or anyone else; it's to verbalize my challenges as I meet them and to weigh all my options. Writing in the journals is a warm-up, the repository for my research, dialogue fragments, and character sketches. There have been times when I've lifted entire paragraphs from a journal and stitched them into the scene I'm writing, which always feels like a gift.

The six working journals for *V Is for Vengeance* totaled 967 single-spaced pages. The finished manuscript was 662 double-spaced pages. This might appear to represent a whole lot of wasted effort. But in truth, every wrong turn eventually led to the right one. In the end, I wouldn't have given up a single moment of the process.

Eudora Welty once said, "Every book teaches you the lessons necessary to write that book." To which I add, "The problem is that the lessons learned from writing one book seldom apply to the next."

Father knew best

I was raised in a household where reading and the love of good literature were an essential part of our daily lives. My father, C. W. Grafton, was a municipal bond attorney. He wrote mysteries in his spare time, if lawyers can be said to have spare time. He'd put in a full day's work as a lawyer, come home for supper, and then go back to his office to write.

After years of doing this, he managed to publish two novels of what he intended to be an eight-book series, *The Rat Began to Gnaw the Rope* and *The Rope Began to Hang the Butcher*. He borrowed the titles from an English nursery rhyme about an old lady trying to get a pig over a stile. (These days, there's probably not a kid in this world who knows what a "stile" is, unless it's mentioned in the same sentence with Juicy Couture.)

When my father realized he couldn't make a living wage from his writing, he was forced to set aside his series in order to support his wife and two daughters. His intention was to go back to writing when he retired, but he died before he was able to do that.

As I was growing up, my father talked often and lovingly about the process of writing. Those lessons sifted down into my consciousness long before it occurred to me that I might write one day. His passion for the mystery genre was something I picked up at an early age.

I wasn't cut out to be a ballerina

When I was growing up long, long ago, girls had limited career options. In alphabetical order, the choices were: ballerina, nurse, salesclerk, secretary, stewardess, or teacher.

I had no physical talents whatever, so there went *Swan Lake*. I suspected that teaching, which is extremely fulfilling for some people, would be a bore for me. I was married and a young mother, so Pan Am was out of the question. I was interested in medicine, although perhaps not for the loftiest of reasons. When I was in my early twenties, the two most popular television series were *Dr. Kildare* and *Marcus Welby, M.D.* In my fevered imagination, I conjured myself in a white cap, white shoes, and a crisp white uniform, awash in purity of purpose, sacrifice, dedication, drama, emergencies, lives saved, and all made right with the world. How much better could a job be?

Unfortunately, I'm squeamish about blood and suffering. I'm also needle-phobic. So becoming a nurse in real life meant I'd actually spend my days stretched out on the floor in a dead faint.

I've mentioned the sorry results of my dreams of working at Sears. So my last hope rested on my untapped secretarial aspirations. Hell, I was game. I taught myself how to type, pretended I knew medical terminology, and got a job as an admissions clerk, and then as a secretary, in a hospital clinic for the indigent. Later, I processed applications and typed up intern and resident rotations in a hospital. Later still, I ran the front office for a family physician. All of this, please note, in the white uniform and white shoes I'd originally pictured myself wearing.

After work every night I'd come home, cook supper, wash dishes, chat with my then-husband, and put the children to bed. Then I'd sit down at my desk where I wrote from nine p.m. until midnight. Within the space of four years, I'd finished three full-length novels, which never saw the light of day. The fourth, *Keziah Dane*, was published in 1967 when I was twenty-five years old. My advance was fifteen hundred dollars. I thought I'd died and gone to heaven.

Doctor of literature

Mystery writers are the neurosurgeons of literature. Or maybe magicians. We work by sleight of hand.

Constructing a credible detective story takes ingenuity, patience, and skill. The writer has to find the perfect balance between right brain, the creative function, and left brain, the analytical. We have to develop character and plot at the same time—and by "plot" I'm not talking about a formula. Plotting is the way a story proceeds. It's the sequence of events that unfolds and builds, scene by scene, to a satisfying conclusion.

A mystery is the only literary form that pits the reader and the writer against each other. The writer's side of the deal is to play fair. That means letting the reader make the same discoveries the detective makes in any given moment, putting all the information on the table in plain view.

The trick is to conceal one's purpose, distracting the reader's attention while laying out the bits and pieces that will eventually point to the resolution. If a story's too convoluted, the reader gets annoyed by having to keep track of unnecessary or implausible twists and turns. If a story's too simple, and the answer to the question of "whodunit" is obvious, the reader's annoyed because that takes away the pleasure of outsmarting the writer, who's trying to pull the wool over the reader's eyes.

The fact that any mystery writer succeeds at this impossible commission can only be described as miraculous.

Sue Grafton's Wisdom for Writers

- There are no secrets and there are no shortcuts. As an aspiring writer, what you need to know is that learning to write is self-taught, and learning to write *well* takes years.

- You've got to write and revise every sentence, every paragraph, and every page over and over until the rhythm, the cadence, and tone are properly attuned to your inner ear.

- Figuring out how to get an agent, how to find a publisher, how to write a good query letter, how to pitch, how to network—all of this is beside the point until you've mastered the craft and honed your skills. Banging out a single book, then thinking you're ready to give up your day job and be a full-time writer, is the equivalent of learning to play "Three Blind Mice" on the piano and expecting to be booked into Carnegie Hall.

CHAPTER SIX

Sara Gruen

The plane had yet to take off, but Osgood, the photographer, was already snoring softly. He was in the center seat, wedged between John Thigpen and a woman in coffee-colored stockings and sensible shoes. He listed heavily toward the latter, who, having already made a great point of lowering the armrest, was progressively becoming one with the wall. . . .

—Opening lines, *Ape House*, 2010

Have you heard the one about the writer who sits down at her desk, scratches out a first novel, and hits the jackpot overnight? Sales in the millions, legions of adoring fans, wealth, fame, a movie deal that *actually results in a movie*, a staff to regretfully decline an endless stream of glamorous invitations?

That was Sara Gruen's story, I thought, and I told her so. Laughing uproariously, she corrected my misperception in her Canadian accent. *Water for Elephants* (which has sold more than five million copies in fifty-seven languages and was made into a 2011 movie starring Reese Witherspoon) has earned Gruen pretty much all of the jackpot items above—minus the staff. Her husband works full-time as her manager. But *Water for Elephants* was her third book, not her first. And the first two were merely "moderately successful." And *Elephants* was rejected by the publisher of her first two novels. It sold to another publisher, after four months of rejections, for a very modest price.

"*Water for Elephants* came within fifteen minutes of not selling at all," Gruen told me. Jackpot notwithstanding, there was an unmistakable ring of gratitude in her voice.

THE VITALS

Birthday: July 26, 1968

Born and raised: Born in Vancouver, British Columbia; raised in London, Ontario

Current home: Asheville, North Carolina

Love life: Married to former book editor and creative writing professor Robert C. Gruen

Family life: Three sons, ages 10, 13, and 17

Schooling: Graduated from Carleton University, Ottawa, with highest honors in English literature, 1993; honorary doctorate of humane letters, Wittenberg University, 2011

Day job?: Worked as a technical writer until 2001; now writes fiction full-time

Honors and awards (partial listing): Book Sense Book of the Year Award, 2007; *Cosmo*'s Fun Fearless Fiction Award; BookBrowse Diamond Award for most popular book; Friends of American Literature Adult Fiction Award; Alex Award, 2007

Notable notes:

- Along with her husband and children, Sara Gruen shares her home with three dogs, four cats, two budgies, two horses, a goat, and a fish.
- Gruen is a dual citizen of Canada and the United States.
- Even as a technical writer, Gruen needed so much privacy to write that she had extra walls put up around her cubicle.
- Thanks to international sales of her books, Gruen is a taxpayer in 57 countries.

Website: www.saragruen.com

Facebook: www.facebook.com/profile.php?id=654617064&sk=wall

Twitter: @saragruen

THE COLLECTED WORKS

Novels

Riding Lessons, 2004

Flying Changes, 2005

Water for Elephants, 2006

Ape House, 2010

Film Adaptation

Water for Elephants, 2011

Sara Gruen

Why I write

The only thing that makes me crazier than writing is not writing.

I knew I wanted to be a writer as soon as I knew how to

read, and I began by making little illustrated books. At age seven, I sent one to a publisher. I've always been a stickler for detail, so I folded all the pages in half and stapled them carefully from the inside so it was nicely bound. I got a letter back from the editor—a rejection, of course. But I was thrilled. I have no idea what happened to the letter. I suspect it's in my mother's attic.

I was twelve when I wrote my first "novel." It was about a girl who wakes up and a horse has jumped into her backyard. Lo and behold—the same thing had happened to her neighbor and best friend. It took up three school notebooks. I didn't let anybody read it. I think that book is also in my mother's attic.

I firmly believe that in order to write you must read. My parents had an extensive library, and as a kid I worked my way through it, picking the next book off the shelf when I was done with the last. I read everything from Alexander Pope to Aleksandr Solzhenitsyn.

Besides having a great library, one of the best things my parents did for my career was to make me take typing in high school. I can type as fast as I can think, which is crucial when the story's flowing. I've been clocked at an honest 120 words a minute. Not coincidentally, nobody, including me, can read my handwriting. I've more or less given up on it.

There's a moment in every book when the story and characters are finally *there*; they come to life, they're in control. They do things they're not supposed to do and become people they weren't meant to be. When I reach that place, it's magic. It's a kind of rapture.

I would write even if I couldn't make a living at it, because I can't not write. I am amazed and delighted and still in a state of shock about the success of *Water for Elephants*, but that's not why I write. I do it for love. The rest is gravy.

How I write: through a portal darkly

When I write, I have to be entirely by myself. I just had an office built in our house, and it's the first time I've ever had a room with a door, or even a room.

When I first started writing I had a corner in the living room. I put up a freestanding screen, but that didn't keep little bodies from coming around the corner and asking for cookies. I could only write when no one else was home. We ran out of money for day care when my first book didn't sell, so all of a sudden I was taking care of a toddler and trying to write. My husband built me an office—really more of a cage—out of baby gates. My son couldn't unplug the computer anymore, but he could still throw things at me. Somehow I managed to finish my second book, and when it sold, we could afford a babysitter and once again I had the house to myself during the day.

That didn't always translate into productivity. At one point, I was so stuck on *Water for Elephants* that I worked in a walk-in closet. I covered over the window and made my husband move his clothes out and pasted pictures of old-time circuses on the walls. We had no Wi-Fi, which was perfect. The only thing I could do was open my file. I figured if I stared at it long enough, something would happen. Apparently I was right, because I finished the book, but I spent four months in that closet. Does a walk-in closet count as a room of one's own? Somehow I don't think it's what Virginia Woolf had in mind.

My writing process is embarrassingly ritualistic. When I'm

beginning a new book, I steep in the idea until the first scene comes to me whole. I go to sleep thinking about it, I'm thinking about it when I shower, when I cook. During that period I walk into a lot of walls.

Once I'm actually writing, my days all look the same. After I drink my tea, check my e-mail, and let the birds out, I open my file and read what I wrote the day before, over and over, until I feel I can continue. It usually takes me an hour and a half, but at some point I feel like I've gone through a portal into that other world, the fictional world, and I'm recording what's going on rather than creating it.

If I answer the phone, or someone comes to the door, the spell is broken. Then I have to do that one-and-a-half-hour trance thing all over again. That's why my office is at the back of the house, and that's why the door is so important: there are only so many hour-and-a-halves in a day. If my door is closed, nobody knocks. I'm not proud of it, but once, when I still only had a corner in the living room, I hid behind the curtains from the mailman.

"I need a job, and I want to be a ~~paperback~~ technical writer"

I moved to the States from Canada in 1999 for a tech writing job. I liked it. It was a way I could write and get paid for it. When I got laid off in 2001 I was devastated. The longer you're with a company, the closer you get to a window. At any new job, I was going to be right back by the elevator shaft.

My husband and I had talked about me retiring early to try writing fiction. I'd had delusions of writing a novel during my first maternity leave, but that was because I didn't actually know what newborns were like. Or novels. Needless to say, that didn't work. So when I got laid off we decided we'd give it two years or two books, whichever came first. If I hadn't replaced my salary as a tech writer by then, I'd go back to tech writing. We'd set ourselves up as a two-income family. We had a mortgage. We had three kids. We basically held hands and jumped off the cliff.

A quiet little book

At the two-year (and two-book) mark, *Riding Lessons* sold. It was a moderate success, by which I mean nobody cared what I was doing for the next year. What I was doing for the next year was writing *Water for Elephants*.

I submitted *Elephants* to my editor, and she turned it down. But in the same e-mail she asked me to do a sequel to *Riding Lessons*. So I turned around and wrote *Flying Changes*. While I was doing that, my agent sent *Water for Elephants* out to other publishers. Nobody even looked at it for the longest time. After four and a half months, somebody at Random House finally pulled it out of the pile, read it, and liked it. At that point, my agent called the other editors and said, "We have interest." Then all the editors started reading, and I got the strangest rejections. I kept hearing things like "Thank you for letting us look at this historical romance," and "Circus books don't sell." I thought, "What circus books? I can't think of a single one."

Finally in 2006 we sold it for a very small advance. My income had gone down steadily and dramatically for each of my three books. The editor who bought *Elephants* initially thought of it as a quiet, good book. A little book. But the country's independent booksellers had other ideas. They refused to let *Water for Elephants* fail. When customers walked into their stores, they thrust my book into their hands. They made it the Book Sense Book of the Year. On the sheer strength of the indies, the chains had to buy it. It hit the *New York Times* bestseller list three or four weeks after it was published. A friend of mine who saw me around that time told me I looked shell-shocked. Which was exactly how I felt.

The dread follow-up novel

The hardest time I've ever had as a writer was writing *Ape House*. Before you're published, there's a sense of freedom in that nobody knows who you are or expects anything from you. I never expected *Water for Elephants* to be so successful, but it was, and I was moving forward with the knowledge (and fear) that a lot of people were going to read the next book. I had to find a way to become unaware, which was difficult because I was still doing a lot of public events for *Elephants*.

I had to get off the road. I had to be on my own and pretend that nobody had ever heard of me. I had to open my file and go through the portal and get into that place and not worry about what potential readers might think. It was very, very hard. I had to turn down invitations and I felt guilty, but I can't travel for one book and write another at the same time. I just can't. There is only room for one fictional world in my head at a time.

Also—and I think this must happen in every field—there's a lot of schadenfreude in this business. I knew there would be people gunning for me, and I was right. Sure, I got reviewed in the *New York Times Book Review*, but it was a nasty, almost personal, review.

The pressure is gone now. I've done my postbreakout book, and I survived. And I'm pretty damned proud of the book, too.

Why did the chick lit cross the road?

There are very good, very successful authors of "chick lit" and "women's fiction," but that's not how I self-identify. I think if you're a woman and you write novels with female characters, the industry tends to pigeonhole you, and if you're not careful you get slapped with a pink cover no man would be caught dead reading on a subway. Why would I want to discount male readers? I want men *and* women to feel they can pick up my books.

I felt (correctly) that I was labeled as a women's fiction author with *Riding Lessons*, and I hate very little as much as I hate being labeled. So I very deliberately wrote *Water for Elephants* as a book that would be difficult to classify. I figured that having it narrated by a ninety-three-year-old man would help. And what do you know? I think it did.

Me and my magic rocks

I'm a little bit superstitious. As I said, everything I do with my writing is ritualized. After I check my e-mail, I get another cup of tea. I check my e-mail again. And then I shut down the Internet and open my file. Actually, I do more than shut down the Internet. I use an app called Freedom to block me from it. Of course, I've figured out how to get around it, so when I'm really desperate, I get my long-suffering husband to change the network password and I tell him not to give me the new one until the end of the day. Was it Trollope who had his housekeeper chain him to his desk with strict orders not to release him despite all pleas and threats until a set time? Maybe it was Stevenson. Anyway, this feels similar.

I clean my office completely before I start each book. Pretty normal so far, right? Well, I also have a collection of colorful rocks and a golden horseshoe, and every time I start a book I have to put my horseshoe down and arrange my stones within it until it feels right. And then I don't touch them again until I finish the book. If I feel the need to rearrange the rocks while I'm writing, that's a symptom of a pretty bad block.

I also never actually delete anything I write. If I know a paragraph, page, chapter, or scene has to go, I put it in a file called "Leftovers." I've never recycled a single word from that file, but it's one of those silly mental crutches that allows me to get rid of stuff. And getting rid of stuff is half the battle.

Sara Gruen's Wisdom for Writers

- Planning and plotting and research are all fine. But don't just think about writing. Write!

- Opening yesterday's file can be the hardest part of a writer's day. But that's what writing is: building a bunch of yesterday's scribblings into the book of today or tomorrow.

- It's hard to find time to write, especially when you have a job or kids, or both. Tell the people who love you that your writing time is sacred. And even if it's two hours on a Saturday, take that time.

CHAPTER SEVEN

Kathryn Harrison

Behold: in the beginning there was everything, just as there is now. The giant slap of a thunderclap and, bang, *it's raining talking snakes.*

A greater light to rule the day, a lesser light to rule the night, swarming water and restless air. A man goes down on two knees, a woman opens her thighs, and both hold their breath to listen. Imagining God's footsteps could be heard in the cool of the day. . . .

—Opening lines, *Enchantments*, 2012

In 1992, reading the first line of Kathryn Harrison's first novel—*In truth, my mother was not a beautiful woman*—I felt I'd found the author I'd been waiting for all my reading life. Who'd claimed that the narrator's mother *was* a beautiful woman? I wondered. Who was this authoritative child-narrator, arguing that she was not?

Booklist once called Kathryn Harrison's work "diabolically compelling." Unfortunately but unsurprisingly, Harrison is best known for her memoir *The Kiss*, an exploration of her four-year sexual relationship with her father, beginning when she was twenty. To label Harrison the Writer Who Slept with Her Father is like labeling Sylvia Plath the Writer Who Killed Herself. But the sales and controversy generated by *The Kiss* placed Kathryn Harrison where she belongs: on the short list of fearless, brilliant modern American writers to watch, a writer who turns readers into fanatical fans and fans like me into writers who look to her for courage and inspiration.

THE VITALS

Birthday: March 20, 1961

Born and raised: Los Angeles, California

Current home: Brooklyn, New York

Love life: Married to writer and editor Colin Harrison since 1988

Family life: Sarah (1990), Walker (1992), Julia (2000)

Schooling: BA in English and art history, Stanford, 1982; MFA, Iowa Writers' Workshop, 1987

Day job?: Teaches memoir writing at Hunter College

Notable notes:

- Kathryn Harrison's parents married at 17, when her mother found out she was pregnant, and separated before Harrison was one year old. She was raised by her maternal grandparents and didn't see her father again until she was 20.
- Harrison's grandmother was raised and lived in Shanghai, which inspired Harrison's novel *The Binding Chair*. Her British grandfather was a fur trapper in Alaska, which provided the impetus for *The Seal Wife*.

- *New York Times* book critic Michiko Kakutani called *The Binding Chair* "mesmerizing."

Website: www.kathrynharrison.com

Facebook: www.facebook.com/profile.php?id=646167544

Twitter: nope

THE COLLECTED WORKS

Novels	Nonfiction
Thicker Than Water, 1992	*The Kiss*, 1997
Exposure, 1993	*The Road to Santiago*, 2003
Poison, 1995	*Saint Thérèse of Lisieux*, 2003
The Binding Chair, 2000	
The Seal Wife, 2002	*Seeking Rapture*, 2003
Envy, 2005	*The Mother Knot*, 2004
Enchantments, 2012	*While They Slept*, 2008

Kathryn Harrison

Why I write

I write because it's the only thing I know that offers the hope of proving myself worthy of love. It has everything to do with my relationship with my mother. I spent my childhood in an attempt to remake myself into a girl she would love, and I've translated that into the process of writing—not intentionally, but just as I was always looking beyond my present incarnation toward the one that would woo my mother's attention, I'm always looking toward the book that hasn't come out yet: the one that will reveal me as worthy of love.

I was a neurotic schoolgirl. I got straight A's from seventh to twelfth grade, and I was class valedictorian. My grandfather offered to give me ten dollars for every A I earned. I said, "I'm not selling those A's." My schoolwork was the only place I felt was mine. I was in control there as I was nowhere else in my life. It taught me to be diligent, to come home and do my homework. I'm still a schoolgirl. I love the research, the homework of writing a book.

I'd planned to go to med school. I had countless fantasies of my glorious career as a physician, but once I was in college, studying art history, and I discovered that one could sit in the dark and look at beautiful things and write about them, I was irrevocably set on that path.

When it's great, writing can be ecstatic. Even when it's just hard, it's always involving. The moments that are sublime—I get just enough of them that I don't lose hope of being given another—are only so because for that moment, when even as little as a sentence seems exactly right, before the feeling fades, it offers what I think it must feel like to be worthy of love. I want praise, of course; it's a cousin of love. But equally important to me is a bit of evidence, here and there, that a reader got it, saw what I'd hoped to reveal.

I write, also, because it's the apparatus I have for explaining the world around me, seemingly the only method that works. By the time I was in high school I'd discovered that the process of hammering text on the page—being able to articulate things, to get them right—offered not only consolation but a place I could live inside. Before there were thumb drives, I always carried the hard copy of what I was working on with me. I couldn't leave the house without it. If the house burned down, I thought, I still have this. This is really where I live.

Writing is a lonely job. You have to be willing to work for months and months without anyone saying, "You're doing well; keep going." You have to be willing to live in a constant state of uncertainty. Not very many personalities are well suited for it. Fortunately, mine is.

When I'm in the midst of a book, that's all I am: the person working on *Enchantments*. When I lose that connection I'm unmoored for a while. I have trouble letting go of one book before becoming wedded to another. I have any number of aborted manuscripts that I realize, in retrospect, were intermediary masks to hide behind before I got going on the book I was meant to write. Until I get traction with a new book, I can't not write a fake book.

One thing I love about writing is that in that moment, I am most completely myself, and yet totally relieved of my self. I don't really like spending that much time with myself when I'm not writing, but when I'm in that strange paradox of being most and least myself, I can be transcendently happy, rapturous. Those moments are rare—I'm doing really well if it's two percent of the time—but memorable, like a drug high you have to get back to.

When you write, endless possibility exists before you. The unwritten sentence—perhaps that will be the one, the one that makes life comprehensible, the one that reveals the beauty and order under what can sometimes seem like a landscape of chaos and cruelty. Whenever someone asks me which book is my best, I say I hope it's the one I'm writing now. If what I have yet to write didn't beckon with promise, I'd have no inducement to write—let alone the pressure that drives me to hammer and hammer at something until it seems acceptable, good enough for the moment, anyway, enough to be revisable in a day or a month. And so, no matter that it's characterized more often by a feeling of failure than of success, I am dependent on it.

For me, writing is inseparable from thinking. I could say the entire undertaking is a vast cerebral construct against my demons. It's the thing that I love. It's my identity.

Where I write

My study is like a reliquary. I have no family of origin anymore; whatever remains of it fills the shelves and lines the walls of my office: touchstones, my favorite books, the orchids my mother used to grow in my study window in their special light. Every inch of wall is covered with portraits of my family, and portraits my older daughter, an artist, painted. I'm always happy to step into my study. I come here for solace even when solace isn't available.

How I write

I get off on index cards. It's pathetic but true. There's nothing that looks better to me than a stack of index cards with a pen beside it. On my desk right now I have a pile of blanks and a pile I've already scribbled on, waiting to be filed in what looks like a glorified recipe box. For the book I'm working on now, the dividers in the box say "Prophesy," "Enunciation," "Crown-ing," "Betrayal," "Martyrdom."

Writing is strangely tiring for something that doesn't in-volve moving a muscle. It requires an enormous amount of psy-chic energy. By the end of the day I'm shot—in a good way.

I can get really tense while I'm writing. As I get more fa-tigued, the tension builds in my body. My jaw gets so clenched, I once broke a molar while I was working. Over the decades I've learned what to do to offset some of the stress. My body pretty much follows along with my head. If I leave my desk happy with the day, I'm ready to let it go.

Let us now praise dirty soccer uniforms

God knows what would happen if I lived without people who need things from me. I'd be some kind of monster if there was no dinner to be made, no soccer uniform to be washed. I'd be the monkey who keeps taking coke until his head explodes.

My husband and I met in grad school, at the Iowa Writers' Workshop. He could see immediately that I wasn't somebody who should be living alone. My fridge was always empty. I have no talent for self-preservation. I owe my stability to the people I care about. There's no going off the rails when you have chil-dren. I don't know how much work I'd get done without my family to keep me in line.

When he married me, my husband knew he had somebody on his hands with a lot of baggage. He's a pretty intuitive man. He understood that there were limited ways in which I could keep myself stitched together, and writing was one of them.

Writing is a job. If you're going to do a job, you're going to do it every day. You're going to get enough sleep, and not fall into dissolute habits. I never had a romantic idea about writing. In grad school other people would spend the evening drinking, then tear home to write something at three in the morning, thinking the work would be exceptional because of the exceptional circumstances under which it had been produced. You don't write by sitting in a garret thinking the muse might arise under some particular circumstances.

The thirty-six-hour day

During the late 1980s, I worked as a book editor at Viking Penguin. I loved the job. It was very interesting, and it was useful for me to get over what had previously seemed a fortified wall between publishing and writing. It demystified the process of publishing a book, which I think is a very good thing. But, after I'd been working at Viking for six months or so, my husband said, "This is really stupid. You're working on other people's writing instead of your own." So I began getting up at five in the morning, to write until seven, when I got ready for work. That's how I wrote my first novel.

When I finished it, I showed it to an editor I'd worked with at Viking. She told me to send it to Amanda (Binky) Urban, one of the most powerful agents in New York. I was terrified, but I did. Two days later I got a call from Binky's assistant, saying Binky wanted to see me. I hadn't expected her to take me on as a client—my fear was that Binky had summoned me to her office to chastise me in person for having the audacity to approach her. I'd been working at Viking for a couple of years, and was about nine months pregnant, when I appeared in Binky's office.

She greeted me by reading me the list of editors to whom she was going to send my manuscript. She said she was going to hold an auction. I sat there gravidly, dumbly nodding. When I left I called my husband. He asked what happened, and I told him I wasn't sure. He said, "Is Binky Urban your *agent*?" I said I guessed she was, but I'd been so certain of rejection that I just didn't believe it. I went back to my desk at Viking. That was on a Friday. The following Monday, Binky called and said she had a preemptive offer from a big editor at Random House. I'd been preparing myself for years of rejection. I wasn't prepared to be handed a golden ticket to skip over all of that.

My grandmother was living with us at the time, and by the time the book went into production I had a baby on my hands as well. I needed thirty-six hours in a day, and my husband was now working as an editor while writing a novel, but we both knew he doesn't need writing in the same way that I do. So he kept his job and I quit mine. It was scary to leave an office with colleagues and regular paychecks. It was a gamble, and it paid off—that was in 1990, twelve books ago.

Headiest experience

The best and the worst, the most exciting and most awful experience I've had as a writer was working on *The Kiss*. I wrote it after spending years in psychoanalysis, trying to understand what had happened between (among) my mother, my father, and me. What I wanted—what I thought I wanted—was something like a pie graph revealing each of our slices of culpability.

Finally I had this shining moment of clarity. I realized I'd reached an impasse, that assigning blame wouldn't help me to tell the story. I saw who we were, my mother, my father, myself, and I thought, I can just write about what happened. I can try to reveal what happened in ways that make it an understandable story, even if it's not one anyone wants to hear.

Once I started, I realized I'd been writing *The Kiss* in my head for a decade. There were sentences I'd revised more than once without ever writing them down. It spilled out of me, not without effort, but in a white heat. I woke up at three every morning, got my kids to school at seven, went back to my desk till they got home at three thirty, and went back there after they were in bed and wrote till midnight. I'd lie down next to my husband for a few hours, then get up and start again. I was afraid that if I stopped I might not keep going.

When the book was published, it sparked a huge debate about what was okay to write about. I believe that you can write about anything. Nothing should be excluded from the world of books; that's what books are for. But I got reviews whose last words were "shut up."

It was very difficult to be pilloried in public. I read my reviews because I'm always looking for constructive criticism, but the reviews of *The Kiss* exposed me to things that were really ugly: character assassination, slander.

I understand myself to be a writer who people aren't tepid about. People tend to really like my work or find the subjects I choose—the ones that choose me—offensive. I like being that writer, not the writer whose work you read and forget.

I like to hit a nerve. I like to hear from some people that a book of mine saved their lives and hear from others, "You ought to be locked up." Tepid responses make me feel I've failed somehow. I don't portray myself as who I want to be. I portray myself as who I am.

If *The Kiss* had been written by a man; if my father, say, had written about us, he might not have been attacked, as I was, for being honest about a shameful thing. I came out of that publication banged up, but it was a good thing for me overall. I realized that I couldn't do anything to make people say anything worse about me than they'd already said. So it was freeing.

Kathryn Harrison's Wisdom for Writers

- At the end of a workday, leave yourself a page marker, an instruction that tells you where to start the next morning, so you're oriented immediately when you sit down at your desk.

- We all know talented people who piss their lives away, and dogged souls who show up even when they're un-inspired, even when they've lost faith in their work. It's good to have talent *and* discipline, but there's really no substitute for self-discipline.

- Don't portray yourself as who you want to be. Portray yourself as who you are.

CHAPTER EIGHT

Gish Jen

It's the băi shù *you'd notice most—the thousand-year-old cypresses—some of them upright, some of them leaning. And their bark, you'd see, if you visited—upward-spiraling, deeply grooved, on these straight trunks that rise and rise. They look as though someone took a rake to them, then gave them a twist, who knows why.*

—Opening lines, *World and Town*, 2010

✧

"Jen knows how to create thoughtful characters who can talk and think about complex issues without making us take notes," *Washington Post* reviewer Ron Charles wrote about *World and Town*. In her review of *The Love Wife*, *New York Times* critic Michiko Kakutani wrote, "Ms. Jen takes big social issues like ethnic identity and racial prejudice and filters them through the prism of . . . individuals so in thrall to their own quirky emotional histories that they never for a moment seem like generic or representative figures."

A second-generation Chinese American whose parents immigrated to the United States in the 1940s, novelist Gish Jen has built a career on craft and contradiction. The pure

power of her prose has earned her a devoted following of die-
hard fans and a slew of rave reviews and awards, including a
Strauss Living from the American Academy of Arts and Letters. And, while challenging some of America's most entrenched melting-pot myths as only an insider/outsider could,
she has somehow managed to defy categorization as an "immigrant novelist."

THE VITALS

Birthday: August 12, 1955

Born and raised: Long Island, Queens, and Scarsdale, New
York

Current home: Boston, Massachusetts

Love life: Married

Family life: Two children

Schooling: BA from Harvard, 1977; MFA from Iowa Writers' Workshop, 1983

Day job?: No

Honors and awards (partial listing): Grants from the Guggenheim Foundation, the Radcliffe Institute for Advanced
Study, the National Endowment for the Arts, and the Fulbright Commission; a Strauss Living from the American
Academy of Arts and Letters; a Lannan Literary Award;
member of the American Academy of Arts and Sciences

Notable notes:

- Gish Jen's birth name, and the name under which she published her first story, Lillian Jen. Her film buff classmates
in high school nicknamed her "Gish" after Lillian Gish.

- Jen was premed at Harvard, considered going to law school, and realized she wanted to study writing while enrolled in Stanford Business School.
- Jen didn't have access to a library until she was in fifth grade, when her family moved from Queens to Scarsdale.

Website: www.gishjen.com

Facebook: www.facebook.com/pages/gish-jen/1120204221 48586

THE COLLECTED WORKS

Novels

Mona in the Promised Land, 1996

The Love Wife, 2004

Typical American, 2007

World and Town, 2010

Fiction Collection

Who's Irish? short stories, 1999

Periodicals

The New Yorker

The Atlantic Monthly

The New York Times

The Los Angeles Times

The New Republic

Gish Jen

Why I write

Writing is part and parcel of how I am in the world. Eating, sleeping, writing: they all go together. I don't think about why

I'm writing any more than I think about why I'm breathing. Its absence is bad, just as not breathing would be bad.

When I'm writing I'm unaware of myself. I'm in my characters, in the story. I know the writing is going well when I look at my watch and see that it's ten p.m., and the last time I looked it was noon.

My writing has always been very intuitive. When I start a piece I don't have a plan; I'm not looking ahead. I'm looking only at what I'm doing, and then I look up and realize, Here I am at the other shore of the lake, so I guess I must have been swimming.

Why I'm not supposed to write

Even a lot of second-generation Asian Americans are uncomfortable talking about ourselves and taking up a lot of room. From birth we've been encouraged to think about ourselves in terms of our social roles, so when we talk about our childhoods, some of us talk about our own childhoods, but some of us talk more about others than we do about ourselves.

The whole question of narration for me has been caught up in issues of identity. That's one of the reasons I was so slow coming to the idea of writing.

Books were precious to me as a child because we didn't have a lot of them. My parents didn't read to me, and I went to a Catholic school that only had a donated library. My godmother would send me books for Christmas, though: *Heidi*, *Little Women*. I read them each thousands of times.

Versification

When I was a junior in college, I took a writing class by acci-
dent. It was a class on prosody, taught by Robert Fitzgerald, the
translator. I signed up for it because I felt I didn't understand
poetry. Why did poems have those little lines? Why didn't po-
ets just say what they meant? I didn't understand from the
course description that I was actually myself going to have to
write poetry in this class, but when the light went on, I thought,
well, let me try it; I can always drop the class if it doesn't work
out. So I wrote my first poem, and right away I loved it. I told
my roommate, "If I could do this every day for the rest of my life
I would."

But people like me didn't become writers, and probably I
would not be a writer today had not Fitzgerald said to me,
"Why are you premed? You should do something with words. If
you're not going to be a writer, you should at least be in publishing." He then called up his editor at Doubleday and said, "I've
got this student. You should give her a job."

Today I realize that this didn't happen to everyone, but in
1977 I didn't know enough about the world to be amazed. It
was as if someone had said, "I know this apartment you can
rent"—something helpful, that's all.

Doubleday back then had a program where they'd pay for
any outside courses you wanted to take. So I took a class in
nonfiction writing at the New School, and when I turned in my
assignment the teacher said, "This is the best writing I've seen
in years. You should think about being a writer," about which, I
thought, How strange. Here is another person who thinks I
should be a writer. I started buying literary journals and hang-

ing around with people interested in writing. One of them was Jonathan Weiner, who went on to write *The Beak of the Finch*; back then he was just moving out of poetry and into science writing, which he was very excited about.

After a while it became clear that by working in publishing, I was neither doing what I really wanted to do—which by then, finally, was clearly writing—nor making a reasonable income, and my parents, of course, wanted me to do something practical. My father kept saying, "You have to have a meal ticket"— something, as an immigrant, he understood very well. So I applied to business school, mostly because I'd already been pre-med and prelaw, and B-school was the one sort of grad school I had never considered.

To my amazement, I got into both Harvard and Stanford, and decided to go to Stanford because they had a good writing program there. It was a pretty confusing time, but I took my first fiction classes while I was in business school, and they were wonderful. I took an advanced class first, with Michael Cook. Then I realized that I didn't know the basics, so I backed up and took a beginning class with Stephanie Vaughn. The whole thing was a bit cockamamie, but Michael and Stephanie were truly gifted teachers and taught me a great deal.

I never went to any business classes after the first semester. Instead, I read and read—I think I read a hundred novels that year.

Finally I took a leave of absence and applied to the Iowa Writers' Workshop.

Iowa

This was Iowa in the early 1980s, a much more innocent time. Today there are agents all over the MFA writing programs, but back then, agents were in some far distant future for us. I don't remember anyone discussing agents or how to get one—publishers, either. It was really just about the work.

At Iowa I studied with Barry Hannah, who at one point held a Raymond Carver write-alike contest. It was anonymous; we all signed our entries "Raymond Carver." So the next day, when Barry announced the winner, he had to hold the story up and ask who'd written it. I was mortified to have to raise my hand, and still remember the moment as both happy and awful. Recently someone told me, "You're a very good speaker, but all your stories are about being embarrassed," and I realized that's kind of true. But in any case, there it is.

I published my first story while I was in the program, and under my given name, Lillian Jen. As soon as I saw that "Lillian" I thought, the self who had written the story was not Lillian; and after that, I always published under the name "Gish"—Gish being a nickname I'd picked up in high school.

I don't know which was the chicken and which was the egg, but becoming a writer was very much tied up with taking on this other identity, making up this person who wrote. Lillian was a nice Chinese girl. Gish was not such a nice girl. Gish was the one propping the doors open so I could get back into the dorm at night, the one who got into all kinds of trouble. All these things that were not open to Lillian were open to Gish.

I still think of Lillian as quite a dutiful person. I am a responsible human being. I'm the mother of two, and a more or less upstanding member of society, but there's a kind of freedom that goes with being Gish that didn't go with being Lillian, and that freedom went with writing.

Ninety words per minute

After I got out of Iowa in 1983 I got married and moved east because both my family and my husband's were there. As I needed a job, I thought maybe I should try and get back into publishing. So with the idea I might try for a job at a university press I took a typing test, at the end of which the woman said, "You typed ninety words per minute with no mistakes. I'm sure we can get you a job." I was elated. But in fact she couldn't get me a job at the press or anywhere else. The months went by; and while I was waiting, I got it into my head to apply for a fellowship at the Bunting Institute, though, honestly, I did not think I had any chance of getting one. I was so convinced of this that when they contacted me to say that they were missing a recommendation, I did nothing.

I happened to have lunch around that time with the poet Martha Collins. While we were talking, the subject of my application and my missing recommendation somehow came up, to which she responded, "I'll be your recommender." I said, "I'm not going to get a Bunting," but she marched right over to the Bunting office and said she was my second recommender. And that fall I was a Bunting Fellow at Radcliffe.

My first day was a Monday. I remember everyone sitting in a circle introducing themselves, and when they got to me, I introduced myself as "a would-be writer," to which the other women objected until I finally called myself, for the first time, a writer; and such was the climate of expectation there that by the Friday of that week, I had decided to write a novel. I can still remember writing the first line of the novel that was going to be *Typical American*; I can still see my fingers typing, *It's an American story.*

A number of agents wrote to me as I worked, mostly in response to stories I published here and there; I wrote to them all saying that I'd be in touch once I had a novel, and put their names in a file. And when I was done with my book I got the names back out and sent my book to them, and to my amazement they all liked it. I picked an agent who then found a number of editors who were interested, and we sold it to Seymour Lawrence at Houghton Mifflin. It was all so improbable. In a way, I still can't believe it.

I had a child by then, and knew I needed a place outside the house to work—something I still recommend to young mothers trying to write. In my case, I got a big enough advance to buy myself a small office, a great joy. When I walked into my office for the first time I thought, I am now a permanent resident in the world of literature.

A little enchanted space

My career has been very unusual. I feel incredibly thankful that I am where I am, and extremely dismayed for other writers.

I feel as though I stepped onto a boat that left the dock almost as soon as I stepped onto it. Multiculturalism had a lot of problems, but it did mean that many people wrote who never would have written before. It changed what they wrote about, too.

I've continued in a little enchanted space. I'm at a wonderful publishing house, Knopf, with a wonderful editor, Ann Close. Though I have taken a lot of risks with my work, my house has been with me every step of the way.

Publishing has gotten so much more difficult overall, though. I had a long period of innocence before I quite knew that publishing was a business and books had to be sold. I didn't know what my sales numbers were; that wasn't part of my life. And in truth, I'm still not very clear about them, though I'm not in as much of a fog as I was. But can the young people afford that innocence? I'm aware that this whole project we've embarked upon is fragile and very much at odds with mainstream trends. Anyone who cares about writing has to be more realistic than in the past.

The fact that you can't get an advance you can live on is inevitably going to weed out a lot of good writers. Not that there won't be any; but we will tend, I think, to have writers with both talent and resources. Talent is not going to be enough. Or talent will be enough for the writer to produce one or two books, but not a body of work. And we may well see something like what we see in many elite institutions, too, a kind of barbell, with people with resources doing all right, and people who come from very unrepresented groups also doing unexpectedly well, but with the middle hit hard. As somebody who could so easily have not been a writer myself, I feel terrible to see this happening.

I support every effort to make writing *live* for people—to help people understand how books enrich their lives, and to encourage writers to write books that do actually enrich people's lives. If the crisis in reading helps writers focus on what it is they actually have to say, that will not solve the problem but will still be a good thing.

Gish Jen's Wisdom for Writers

- Writing is a ridiculous thing to do for money. If you do it, do it for the reason writers have always done it, which is not money but for another, deeper satisfaction.

- Readers are interested in what's going on in other parts of the world, because what's going on in other parts of the world is relevant to what's going on here. Writing with an international viewpoint is important.

- When you tell a story in the kitchen to a friend, it is full of infelicities. I try to edit those out in literature but keep the feeling of a story being told. It's not a lecture; it's something much deeper.

CHAPTER NINE

Sebastian Junger

KORENGAL VALLEY, AFGHANISTAN
Spring 2007

O'Byrne and the men of Battle Company arrived in the last
week in May when the rivers were running full and the upper
peaks still held their snow. Chinooks escorted by Apache
helicopters rounded a massive dark mountain called the Abas
Ghar and pounded into the valley and put down amid clouds
of dust at the tiny landing zone. . . .

—Opening lines, Chapter 1, *War*, 2010

N o matter how many more blockbuster books he writes
(he's had four bestsellers to date), or award-winning doc-
umentaries he makes (*Restrepo* won the Sundance Grand Jury
Prize in 2010), Sebastian Junger is likely to be best known, always, for his first book and for its movie adaptation. Who
among us hasn't used the phrase "a perfect storm?" Who among
us can hear that phrase without conjuring George Clooney at
the helm of a tiny, toylike fishing boat being tossed about in the
churl and chop of monster waves?

Another phrase that will be forever associated with Sebastian Junger is "quintessential war reporter." Junger has reported from some of the world's most dangerous war zones, including Nigeria and Afghanistan—where he wrote for *Vanity Fair* and filmed *Restrepo* with his close friend and colleague Tim Hetherington, who was killed by mortar fire in 2011 while reporting from the front lines of the Libyan civil war. About the death of his colleague and dear friend, Junger told me, "There but for the grace of God go I."

THE VITALS

Birthday: January 17, 1962

Born and raised: Belmont, Massachusetts

Current home: New York, New York, and Cape Cod, Massachusetts

Love life: Married since 2005 to writer Daniela Petrova; no kids

Schooling: BA in cultural anthropology, Wesleyan, 1984

Day job?: No

Honors and awards (partial listing): National Magazine Award, 2000; SAIS-Novartis Prize for journalism; PEN/Winship Award; duPont-Columbia Award for broadcast journalism; 2010 Grand Jury Prize: Documentary at the Sundance Film Festival; Oscar nomination for documentary *Restrepo*, 2010

Notable notes:

- All of Junger's books have been *New York Times* bestsellers. *The Perfect Storm* spent more than three years on the bestseller list.

- The Perfect Storm Foundation, founded in 1998, "provides educational opportunities for children of people in the maritime professions."
- Sebastian Junger is co-owner, with fellow author Scott Anderson and filmmaker Nanette Burstein, of the New York restaurant Half King, which serves art exhibits and book readings along with "pub food done right."

Website: www.sebastianjunger.com

Facebook: www.facebook.com/sebastianjunger

Twitter: @sebastianjunger

THE COLLECTED WORKS

Nonfiction

The Perfect Storm, 1997

Fire, 2001

A Death in Belmont, 2006

War, 2010

Film Adaptation

The Perfect Storm, 2000

Documentary

Restrepo, 2010

Magazine Work

Vanity Fair, contributing editor

Harper's

The New York Times Magazine

National Geographic

Outside

Men's Journal

Sebastian Junger

Why I write

When I'm writing, I'm in an altered state of mind.

I'm at my desk. I usually have some music playing, and a cup of coffee. Back when I smoked I had an ashtray and a cigarette; when I was trying to keep from smoking I always had some Nicorette gum in my mouth.

I'm usually not writing fiction, so I'm not wracking my brain for good ideas. My good ideas come from the world. I harvest them but I don't have to think them up. All I have to do is take these things I've seen—things people have said to me, things I've researched, artifacts from the world—and convert them into sequences of words that people want to read. It's this weird alchemy, a kind of magic. If you do it right, it will get read.

When I write a sentence or a paragraph or a chapter that's good, I know it, and I know people are going to read it. That knowledge—Oh my God, I'm doing it, I'm doing this thing again that works—it's just exhilarating. Lots of times I fail at it, and I know it's not good, and it gets deleted.

But when it's good . . . it's like going on a date that's going well. There's an electricity to the process that's exciting and incomparable to anything else.

Up a tree without a paddle

I wrote my first novel in seventh grade—longhand, in a green-and-white composition notebook. My teacher read it aloud to the class, chapter by chapter. No wonder I didn't have any friends.

I didn't give any thought to writing as a profession until the year after I graduated college. I'd written a good thesis; I was on fire the whole time I was writing the thing. I moved to Boston and freelanced once in a while for publications like the *Boston Phoenix*. I got a few short stories published. I got an agent and proceeded to not make a dime for him during the next decade or so. I didn't achieve any kind of critical mass, creatively or financially. I hacked through a lot of underbrush with a dull knife. In a decade of writing I might have made five thousand dollars. I learned what it feels like to work and work and work with no guaranteed outcome. Or no outcome at all!

I did a lot of random jobs, trying to figure out what to do. I worked in a bar. I worked construction. I managed to get a few assignments from the editor of the *City Paper*, and my articles got some attention. Then, in my late twenties, I got a job as a high climber for a tree company. I absolutely loved it. It was amazing work, and potentially very dangerous. You had to be very precise and skilled and monkey-like. I made good money doing it. Some days I made a thousand dollars. Other days I took home a hundred.

When I was thirty I ran into my chainsaw while I was up in a tree and tore up my leg. While I was recuperating, I got this idea to write a book about dangerous jobs. People get killed on low-paid, often disrespected, blue-collar jobs all the time. The country depends on those jobs, and yet we rarely think about the people who do them.

I wrote up a proposal for a book called *The Perfect Storm*, about a fishing boat that sank during a huge storm outside Gloucester, Massachusetts, the town where I lived. I gave the proposal to my agent, and then I went off to Bosnia. I figured that either my agent would sell my book and I'd feel like I'd just slid into home base, or he wouldn't sell it, and I'd become a war reporter. I flew to Vienna and took the train to Zagreb and I hooked up with some freelance writers. I didn't have an assignment. I just had this idea that if you jump off a cliff, you learn to fly.

I landed right in the center of incredible world events. I'd saved up some money and I was living cheaply with other freelancers, sharing expenses. In Zagreb the food is good, the land is gorgeous, the women are very beautiful, and the war had a clear right and wrong. That's about as good as it gets if you're a thirty-year-old guy.

I started filing radio reports—thirty-second voice spots for various radio networks. It paid nothing, but it was legitimate news reporting. I wrote lots of articles, most of which didn't get published. The *Christian Science Monitor* published one.

Then one day in 1994 a guy I was living with tracked me down, yelling, "Hey, man, you got a fax." It was from my agent. I wish I'd saved it. It said, "I sold your book, you've got to come home." I was actually a little disappointed. I didn't want to leave. But he'd gotten me a thirty-five-thousand-dollar advance, so of course I did. I would have written that book for ten bucks.

It took me three years to write it. I was living in my parents' unheated summer house on Cape Cod. I kept doing tree work, because I figured I needed a backup plan.

A perfect storm

There's a bright line in journalism between fact and fiction. I feel very strongly about holding that line. As a journalist, you can't just *imagine* a scene or a conversation.

Halfway through writing *The Perfect Storm* I hit a terrifying dilemma. I was writing a book about a boat that disappeared. As soon as the boat left shore, I lost the thread. What do you say about a boat that disappeared? Where's the action? What are people saying to one another? What does it feel like to die on a ship in a storm? I had a big hole in the middle of my narrative, and I couldn't fill it with fiction.

Everything I know about writing came from reading other people's good work—Tobias Wolff, Peter Matthiessen, John McPhee, Richard Preston. In *The Hot Zone* Preston had faced a similar problem. His central character died, so he had holes in the narrative. He filled them by using the conditional tense. He said to the reader, "We don't know, but maybe he said this, maybe he did that. We know his fever was 106, so he would have felt that."

I realized that I could propose possible scenarios to my readers without lying. As long as I was honest about the fact that these were simply possibilities to be considered, it stayed within the rules of journalism. So I found other boats that had survived a storm and listened to their radio contacts. I could say, "We don't know what happened on my guys' boat, but we know what happened on this other one." I interviewed a guy whose boat had flipped over in heavy seas, and he'd found himself with a lungful of air in a sinking boat. He told me what he thought had happened with the crew of the *Andrea*

Gail, so I could tell that to the reader. I filled the holes legitimately, not with imaginings. Solving that problem was super-exciting for me.

Success brings joy—and misery

The Perfect Storm came out in the spring of '97. The publisher had hopes for it, but no one knew it was going to be as big as it was. It was on the bestseller list for three or four years; it was number one for a while. The movie sold to Warner Bros. for decent money. It felt like doors were just flying open for me. It was a complete writer's fantasy.

I was very proud of the book, but going from being a private person to being in that kind of spotlight was pretty excruciating. I was scared of public speaking, and suddenly I was on a book tour, speaking every day, sometimes in front of thousands of people, absolutely petrified.

The media does this weird thing. If they decide they like you, they paint an unrealistic portrait of you that no one could possibly live up to. I'm five foot eight, and people I met kept saying, I assumed you were six foot three. What was it about my book that made me tall? If you have a healthy amount of insecurity, it gives you a much bigger dose. It caused me to do a lot of painful self-examination. I felt myself shrinking. Every day I was miserable. It never got better.

So I didn't make the mistake of writing a second book right away, which is what everyone expected me to do. I went back to reporting for magazines overseas in Kosovo, Liberia, Kashmir, Afghanistan, Nigeria, Chad, and other places. I was writing about situations that were seriously desperate. What I and other journalists did could potentially save lives by drawing the attention of the world. There were plenty of reporters with more experience, but if I wrote about Sierra Leone in *Vanity Fair*, for example, it often got attention because of my new visibility as an author.

The drug

When I went to Sarajevo in '93 and I was with these other freelance writers, and we were reporting on this incredible story, I went from being a waiter to being a war reporter in the course of three weeks. Seeing your name in print for the first time— nothing can compare to that.

By the time you're at the level where you might be on the *Times* list, it's just part of your business. There are beautiful, beautiful books that never make the list, and there's complete garbage on the list. Every writer knows that. Everyone knows that whether you get on the list, or how long you spend on the list, is not entirely a reflection of the quality of your work.

There are moments in the field, or at your desk, when you can't believe what's flowing through you and coming out on the page. It's the hand of God, or whatever you want to call it: you're writing way beyond yourself.

There are musicians who talk about a solo they've done and they have no idea where that came from. There are athletes who set world records and say, "I performed so far outside my abilities, I don't know what that was." It happens to writers, too. That's the thing we're all looking for. That's the drug. Seeing your name on the *Times* list is such a pale, empty experience compared to that. You can't even compare them.

Writership versus readership

I do this sort of split thing when I'm writing. I'm very aware that I'm writing for readers, and I do everything I can to engage them, to make my writing accessible and compelling.

At the same time, I try to be completely disinterested in what I think people will like. I'm writing for myself. I want to learn about the world, and writing is the way I do it. You can't know people's tastes, anyway. No one could have predicted that *Perfect Storm* would be a hit. A fishing boat that sinks in a storm? The publishers don't know. Readers don't know. Nobody knows.

In every book I've written, there were moments when I thought, I can't put this in, I'll lose half my readership. In *Perfect Storm* it was the physics of wave motion. Who wants to read about that? But I said to myself, The story demands it. Waves sank this boat; you gotta explain how waves work.

So I put the physics in, and I thought, If no one reads it, so be it. If the author thing doesn't work out, I can always go back to tree work. It wouldn't be the end of my life. I'm going to write the best book I can. That said, if I put in a topic I think readers will be resistant to, I work extra hard at my language to make them eat their spinach. I don't like spinach, but if you add enough garlic I'll eat it.

Why I try to write well

Now I know I have an audience, so I feel a huge responsibility to write really well.

When I was writing *War*, I felt such urgency. There had

been a hundred books about the last two wars; who was I to add to the pile? I wanted to write something profound and powerful and useful. Something that people would read. I felt I had to write something extremely profound about the topic.

I wrote *War* in six months. Writing it tapped into something emotional and intuitive in me. I was completely psychologically saturated. I've never had that kind of experience before or since. Every night I was dreaming it; I was back with that platoon. I was also making the movie *Restrepo* about it while I was writing the book.

I've tried to figure out what good writing is. I know it when I read it in other people's work or my own. The closest I've come is that there's a rhythm to the writing, in the sentence and the paragraph.

When the rhythm's off, it's hard to read the thing. It's a lot like music in that sense; there's an internal rhythm that does the work of reading for you. It almost reads itself. That's one of the things that's hard to teach to people. If you don't hear music, you're never going to hear it. That internal rhythm in a sentence or a paragraph, that's the DNA of writing. That's what good writing is.

I pay an awful lot of attention to language. Language is really important to me. It takes longer to write that way, but it's worth it.

Sebastian Junger's Wisdom for Writers

- Don't dump lazy sentences on your readers. If you do, they'll walk away and turn on the TV. You have to earn your paycheck by earning your readers' attention.

- Write for yourself, not for a "market." You can't predict which of your works will connect with the most readers. Some of my best work sold the worst, and vice versa.

- You can't be sloppy about the images you use. If you settle for "the rain hammered down" (which is probably a sentence I've written somewhere or other), it's dead writing. You have to push yourself to think profoundly and imaginatively about what something looks like, what it sounds like, what it feels like. You have to push yourself to find powerful, original ways of describing things.

  If you can do that, and if you have good rhythm in your sentences, people will read everything you write and beg for more.

CHAPTER TEN

Mary Karr

(Prologue: Open Letter to My Son)

Any way I tell this story is a lie, so I ask you to disconnect the device in your head that repeats at intervals how ancient and addled I am. It's true that—at fifty to your twenty—my brain is dimmer. Your engine of recall is way superior, as you've often pointed out. . . .

—Opening lines, *Lit*, 2009

Mary Karr is a writer in possession of a rare and formidable gift. Her prose reads like poetry, and no wonder. Years before *The Liars' Club* landed on the *New York Times* list and stayed there for more than a year, earning Karr a prominent spot in America's literary landscape, she was a published poet. Her plainspoken, devastating poetry made her the recipient of a Guggenheim Fellowship and a Pushcart Prize—not bad for a girl from a southeast Texas refinery town.

In the winter 2009 issue of the *Paris Review*, Amanda Fortini reports on her two-year-long effort to complete her interview with Karr. "She had started [*Lit*] over twice," Fortini wrote, "throwing away nearly a thousand pages, and had been working long hours to meet her deadline."

"It doesn't matter how bleak our daily lives are," Karr told Fortini. "We still fight for the light. I think that's our divinity. We lean into love, even in the most hideous circumstances. We manage to hope."

This is the paradox that powers the words of Mary Karr. She writes from one end of the existential continuum to the other, from the bleak to the divine, from darkness to light.

THE VITALS

Birthday: January 16, 1955

Born and raised: Groves, Texas

Current home: New York, New York

Schooling: Port Neches–Groves High School; Macalester College; MFA from Goddard College, 1979

Day job?: Teaches in English department, Syracuse University

Honors and awards (partial listing): Guggenheim Fellowship; Pushcart Prize; PEN/Martha Albrand Award; Bunting Fellowship; Whiting Writers' Award; National Endowment for the Arts grant

Notable notes:

- At age 11 Mary Karr wrote in her diary: "I am not very successful as a little girl. When I grow up, I will probably be a mess."
- Karr's mentors and teachers include Etheridge Knight, Tobias Wolff, Robert Bly, and Robert Hass.

- Karr's 1991 Pushcart-winning essay, "Against Decoration," in which she argued for direct and clear language in poetry, remains one of her most controversial works.

Website: www.harpercollins.com/author/microsite/about.aspx?authorid=27468

Facebook: www.facebook.com/marykarrlit

Twitter: @marykarrlit

THE COLLECTED WORKS

Memoirs	Poetry
The Liars' Club, 1995	*Abacus*, 1987
Cherry, 2000	*The Devil's Tour*, 1993
Lit, 2009	*Viper Rum*, 2001
	Sinners Welcome, 2006

Mary Karr

Why I write

I write to dream; to connect with other human beings; to record; to clarify; to visit the dead. I have a kind of primitive need to leave a mark on the world. Also, I have a need for money.

I'm almost always anxious when I'm writing. There are those great moments when you forget where you are, when you get your hands on the keys, and you don't feel anything because you're somewhere else. But that very rarely happens. Mostly I'm pounding my hands on the corpse's chest.

The easy times are intermittent. They can be five minutes long or five hours long, but they're never very long. The hard times are not completely hard, but they can be pretty hard, and they can go on for weeks. Working on *Lit*, I threw away two thousand finished pages. Prayer got me through it. That's what gets me through everything.

I usually get very sick after I finish a book. As soon as I put it down and my body lies down and there's not that injection of adrenaline and cortisol, I get sick. I have a medium-shitty immune system so that doesn't help.

All of that said, writing feels like a privilege. Even though it's very uncomfortable, I constantly feel very lucky. For most writers there's a span of twenty years or so when you can't write because you're doing eighty-seven other things. It's really just the past year that I haven't also been raising a kid and teaching. There are more demands on me to do other damn things— touring and lectures—but they're not horrible.

If I couldn't write I'd be very sad. I think I'd do something that had to do with the body. I'd be a yoga teacher or a gym coach or a massage therapist. Of course, none of that would address my need to write. That's why I'm still writing.

Writing drunk, writing sober

I got sober twenty years ago. I wrote my first two books of poetry while I was still drinking. I revised the second one in the loony bin.

I knew I was going to die if I didn't stop drinking. I didn't know how, exactly, but I knew it wouldn't be pretty. I didn't write at all for the first fifteen months I was sober. I couldn't concentrate. Every time I sat down I'd start crying. My mind was too agonizing a place to sit in. It was the struggle not to drink, and also, a lot of feelings came up that I'd been running away from. You know the only way out of those feelings is through them, but you don't have the skill set to get through them. It's trial by fire. People who get sober show more faith than any saint. We step off the cliff into an abyss. It's really dark.

When I went into a mental institution after I stopped drinking, my writing took a great leap forward—or at least people started paying a lot more for it. I was more clear and more openhearted, more self-aware, more suspicious of my own motives. I was more of a grown-up.

I had a spiritual director who was also sober who said to me, "You've tried antidepressants. You've tried psychotherapy. You've tried LSD, cocaine, drinking your brains out. What if the solution to all of your problems was to develop a spiritual practice, and you've never tried it?"

It was seven or eight years after that when I converted to Catholicism. Since then I've been a lot less depressed, a lot less self-centered, believe it or not—as someone who writes memoirs, how dare I say that, but it's true. I'm a lot less worried about my ego, which makes me a better writer.

The myth of the rich and famous author

Before I was a teacher I tended bar. I was a receptionist; I had a strange business career in telecommunications. When I first got sober I was on retainer as an editor with the *Harvard Business Review*. My son's twenty-five, and I started teaching when I was pregnant with him.

I taught a class at Harvard; I got five thousand dollars. I taught a class at Tufts; I got three thousand dollars. I taught a class at Emerson; I got fifteen hundred dollars. For the five years I was teaching in the academic ghetto around Boston, I couldn't live on my earnings. So I continued to write business articles for the *Harvard Business Review*. It didn't help my writing one bit, but it permitted me to keep eating, which permitted me to keep breathing.

I still don't support myself as a writer. I support myself as a college professor. I couldn't pay my mortgage on the revenue from my books. The myth is that you make a lot of money when you publish a book. Unless you write a blockbuster, that's pretty much untrue.

Starting when I was five, I always identified as a writer. It had nothing to do with income. I always told people I was a poet if they asked what I did. That's what I still tell them now.

Unhitching from the plow

For me the best time is at the end of the day, when you've written and forgotten. You wrote longer than you expected to. You've been so absorbed in it that it got late. You unhitch yourself from the plow.

I require myself to do a certain number of hours or pages each day: either six hours or a page and a half. If I've been working all day and I haven't advanced because I keep writing and deleting, then I get to quit after six hours. After that I get up and I go and meet somebody who won't talk to me about the writing. Six hours or a page and a half, whichever comes first.

For *Lit* and *Cherry* at the end it was up to three pages a day, which took me a long time. How much I get done in a day depends on how bad off I am. With *Lit*—I know this sounds insane—I had to do it lying down, because otherwise my back went out. I could lie in bed with this contraption with my laptop on it, and not get a repetitive stress injury.

It wasn't just lying down that made it hard

Lit was the hardest of all the books I've written. You're writing about your kid, your kid's father, spiritual matters in a secular world. Everyone's going to think you're an idiot for becoming a Catholic. You're talking about Jesus. No one's going to be into it.

A lot of reviewers seemed to like those sections. To me that was a triumph. I don't think I converted anybody, but that wasn't my goal. My goal was to describe what a spiritual experience feels like, to re-create the emotional experience of awe when you're not accustomed to it.

God helps

Before I pursue a project, I pray about whether it's what God wants me to do. I don't get written instructions, but I can get a kind of yes or no answer. I'm not like Saint Paul, with God guiding my hand. That would be great, but I don't have that. I'm doing the work just as any writer would. That's why I feel such anxiety and dread.

In the old days, my solution to most problems involved alcohol and firearms. I have very venal, selfish impulses. I need help behaving better than I would normally behave.

At one point I'd been working so hard on *Lit*, and it was so painful, I prayed, "Am I supposed to do this, God, or should I sell my apartment and give the money back?" Obviously I got some kind of yes—from God, from inside me, who knows?

I'm proud of myself for sticking it out and getting it done. I have a sense of pride about it, not based solely on the product, but for having withstood the process. It took a lot of persistence on my part to finish that book. They paid me a lot of money, and I got really great reviews, and I don't have to tell that story anymore. I'm done. It's written.

There are times I ask God to give me the courage to write what's true, no matter what it is. That's no different from Hemingway saying, "I want to write one true sentence." And yeah, people say I'm bullshitting myself about God, but I don't care. It works.

Publishing isn't what it used to be

Currently nobody really knows how to sell books. The whole system is changing, and nobody knows how to make money in this industry in any kind of reliable way.

The industry has this blockbuster mentality that permits a shitty TV star to publish his shitty book and sell three million copies in hardcover, and then you never hear about it again. All the energy is focused on those blockbuster books because they have the most immediate, short-term return.

People have been saying it's the end of the novel since

Hemingway. I don't feel that dire about it. I think more people read than used to read. You have more people reading worse books, but they're still reading books.

I read on my iPad now, and I buy more books than ever. If I like a book I also buy it in cloth or paperback because I want to support the bookstores.

My readers would be shocked to know . . .

. . . how long it takes me to write these books.

I'll look at my students' first drafts, but if a friend says, "I've written eighty pages," and asks me to read them, I'll say, "How many times have you written them?" Because there's usually about one and a half pages worth saving. Most writers aren't willing to part with their own words. Anytime anyone asks me to cut anything, I say, "Great."

Another oddity: if my repetitive stress injury flares up I can really be put out of commission. So I write longhand.

Best time ever? Now.

I just finished writing the lyrics for an album called *Kin*. The musician is Rodney Crowell, a guy who grew up in the same strip of the grain belt that I grew up in. Rodney's been trying to get me to do this for years. Finally I gave in, and we had a ball. I'm very excited about that.

Also, I just sold a TV show called *Lit* to HBO. This woman called me and said she wanted to do a screenplay. She said we could cowrite it, and we did. It was a great experience.

Doing these collaborative things is really fun for me. Writing songs, writing a pilot, anything feels so much easier than writing books. You get way more money and put out way less energy. You're trying to write better than the people who write for TV. That's a really low bar. Plus I'm a freshman, so if I fail it's no big deal.

I was working so hard to get my son through college, but now he's twenty-five and self-supporting. So I only have to teach one semester. I've never had this much free time in my life. I go to the gym every day. It's like the world has just blossomed open.

Mary Karr's Wisdom for Writers

- The quote I had tacked to my board while I was writing *Lit* is from Samuel Beckett, and it's really helpful: "Ever tried. Ever failed. No matter. Try again. Fail better."

- Any idiot can publish a book. But if you want to write a good book, you're going to have to set the bar higher than the marketplace's. Which shouldn't be too hard.

- Most great writers suffer and have no idea how good they are. Most bad writers are very confident. Be willing to be a child and be the Lilliputian in the world of Gulliver, the bat girl in Yankee Stadium. That's a more fruitful way to be.

CHAPTER ELEVEN

Michael Lewis

The willingness of a Wall Street investment bank to pay me hundreds of thousands of dollars to dispense investment advice to grown-ups remains a mystery to me to this day. I was twenty-four years old, with no experience of, or particular interest in, guessing which stocks and bonds would rise and which would fall . . .

—Opening lines, Prologue, *The Big Short*, 2010

I f you haven't seen Michael Lewis on a TV news show (or faux news show) lately, you haven't been watching. A graduate of Princeton and the London School of Economics, the author of several economics-related blockbusters, and a proven financial prognosticator, he's a regular guest on the major networks as well as Bloomberg, Fox, and PBS.

Think he sounds smart, but a bit . . . dry? Think again. Not for nothing does Michael Lewis live in Berkeley with his famous firecracker wife. He's sharp, funny, warm, and irreverent, which also makes him a favored banterer with the likes of Jon Stewart, Rachel Maddow, and Stephen Colbert.

Michael Lewis and Tabitha Soren work in studios connected by a meandering path that circles the wood-frame house where they're raising their three kids. The layout of their sprawling Berkeley hillside compound says it all. Work matters, yes, but family is the center.

Lewis's studio, a 1920s redwood cabin complete with stone fireplace, has the cozy, closed-in feel of a bear's lair, its blinds shut against the bright spring day. "My body clock wants to start writing at midnight and finish at four a.m.," he explained, "but that doesn't work with my kids' schedules. So I have to simulate midnight in the middle of the day."

THE VITALS

Birthday: October 15, 1960

Born and raised: New Orleans, Louisiana

Current home: Berkeley, California

Love life: Married to Tabitha Soren since 1997

Family life: Daughter Quinn born 1999; daughter Dixie born 2002; son, Walker, born 2006

Schooling: BA in art history, Princeton, 1982; master's degree in economics, London School of Economics, 1985

Day job?: Contributing editor, *Vanity Fair*

Notable notes:

- Michael Lewis wrote his first book, *Liar's Poker*, while working full-time at Salomon Brothers.
- Lewis went to the LSE because, after graduating from Princeton, he was turned down by every Wall Street firm to which he applied.

- Lewis takes no advances for his books. He wants to have "some skin in the game" by sharing the investment in his books with his publisher.

(No website, Facebook page, or Twitter account. "I have enough to do.")

THE COLLECTED WORKS

Nonfiction

Liar's Poker: Rising through the Wreckage on Wall Street, 1989

The Money Culture, 1991

Pacific Rift: Why Americans and Japanese Don't Understand Each Other, 1991

Trail Fever: Spin Doctors, Rented Strangers, Thumb Wrestlers, Toe Suckers, Grizzly Bears, and Other Creatures on the Road to the White House, 1997

The New New Thing: A Silicon Valley Story, 2000

Next: The Future Just Happened, 2001

Moneyball: The Art of Winning an Unfair Game, 2003

Coach: Lessons on the Game of Life, 2005

The Blind Side: Evolution of a Game, 2006

Panic: The Story of Modern Financial Insanity, 2008

The Real Price of Everything: Rediscovering the Six Classics of Economics, 2008

Home Game: An Accidental Guide to Fatherhood, 2009

The Big Short: Inside the Doomsday Machine, 2010

Boomerang: Travels in the New Third World, 2011

Michael Lewis

Why I write

When I was at Princeton, I had this very passionate intellectual experience with my senior thesis. I loved writing it. And then I was defending it to my adviser, and he was admiring it—I still have his comments!—but he wasn't saying anything about the quality of the writing. So I asked him, and he said, "I'll put it this way: don't try to make a living at it."

When I got out of Princeton in '82 I was at loose ends. I loved mastering new subjects, and I didn't know how to go on doing that. I wanted to preserve the feeling I'd had, working on my *badly written* thesis, but I had no idea how to make writing an occupation. Then I thought: "I want to be John McPhee."

McPhee taught at Princeton. I never took his class; before I wrote my thesis, I thought I wasn't suited to writing. But he had the life I wanted. He'd go away and research a book every other year, then come back and write it. That seemed like a really good life to me.

When you're twenty-one and loose in the world, you'll try anything. So I wrote a long piece about the homeless people I met at a mission where I was volunteering. And then I bought a copy of the *Writer's Market*, which listed eight thousand publications, and—I don't know what I was thinking—I sent my story to every magazine in it, including in-flight magazines. I got this bewildered letter back from the editor of the Delta magazine, saying, "We admire the effort, but pieces on the life of the underclass in America don't usually run in our publication."

I kept plugging away. I wrote a lot of pieces that never got published. Then, in 1983, I applied for an internship as a science writer at the *Economist*. I didn't get the job—the other two applicants were doing their PhDs in physics and biology, and I'd flunked the one science class I took in college—but the editor who interviewed me said, "You're a fraud, but you're a very good fraud. Go write anything you want for the magazine, except science." They published the first words I ever got into print.

They paid ninety bucks per piece. It *cost* money to write for the *Economist*. I didn't know how I was ever going to make a living at writing, but I felt encouraged. Luckily, I was delusional. I didn't know that I didn't have much of an audience, so I kept doing it.

Then the job on Wall Street fell into my lap, and I thought, There's a living right there. When I took the job, I didn't think I was going to write a book about Wall Street, but it became obvious after a year and a half that I was moving in that direction.

Before I wrote my first book in 1989, the sum total of my earnings as a writer, over four years of freelancing, was about three thousand bucks. So it did appear to be financial suicide when I quit my job at Salomon Brothers—where I'd been working for a couple of years, and where I'd just gotten a bonus of $225,000, which they promised they'd double the following year—to take a $40,000 book advance for a book that took a year and a half to write.

My father thought I was crazy. I was twenty-seven years

old, and they were throwing all this money at me, and it was going to be an easy career. He said, "Do it another ten years, *then* you can be a writer." But I looked around at the people on Wall Street who were ten years older than me, and I didn't see anyone who could have left. You get trapped by the money. Something dies inside. It's very hard to preserve the quality in a kid that makes him jump out of a high-paying job to go write a book. It gets squeezed out of you.

I took a dumb risk, and I never paid a price for that. Instantly I had a book that sold a million copies. Since then it hasn't been a very difficult living at all, but that was fluky.

There's no simple explanation for why I write. It changes over time. There's no hole inside me to fill or anything like that, but once I started doing it, I couldn't imagine wanting to do anything else for a living. I noticed very quickly that writing was the only way for me to lose track of the time. That's not as true anymore as it was when I started, but it still happens, and it's incredible when it does.

It changed, and it changes

The change has less to do with what's inside me than the structure of my life. It's amazing how few demands I had on myself when I was twenty-three years old, and how many I have now. It's just extraordinary. Only by ignoring the vast majority of requests for my time do I have any kind of life at all.

When I was writing my first book, I was going from eleven at night till seven in the morning. I was very happy waking up at two in the afternoon. My body clock would naturally like to start writing around nine at night and finish at four in the morning, but I have a wife and kids and endless commitments. Which is good; I like 'em. I want 'em, and there's a price. I make breakfast. I take the kids to school. My natural writing schedule doesn't work with my family's schedule. I actually do better when I have pressure, some mental deadline.

What disturbs me is that the act of writing is associated with work, rather than pleasure. In the beginning it was associated only with pure pleasure. Now it's a mixture.

The reasons I write change over time. In the beginning, it was that sense of losing time. Now it's changed, because I have a sense of an audience. I have the sense that I can biff the world a bit. I don't know that I have control of the direction of the pinball, but I can exert a force.

That power is a mixed blessing. It's good to have something to get you into the chair. I'm not sure it's great for the writing to think of yourself as important while you're doing it. I don't quite think that way. But I can't deny that I'm aware of the effects my writing will have. It will be read. It will cause some stir.

And money changes it. When I started, I was paid nothing for what I wrote. Now I'm paid vast sums for the worst crap. That's a reason to write now that I didn't have before. Someone will call me up and ask me to write three hundred words. I dash off something in the morning, and I get paid a hundred times what I used to be paid for a piece I'd spend weeks on.

Once you have a career, and once you have an audience, once you have paying customers, the motives for doing it just change.

The other thing that changes is that the threshold that gets me interested in writing about something is higher. When I started, there was nothing I'd have deemed not worth my time as a writer. Now I'm getting choosier and choosier. I'm able to turn things down. And I'm older, so there's less unexplored territory all the time.

Writing makes me sweat

Two things happen to me physiologically when I write that are maybe a little weird. My palms sweat, so my keyboard gets totally wet. Also, my wife says I cackle.

Apparently while I'm writing, I'm laughing hysterically and sometimes talking to myself. Once I was revising a screenplay and Tabitha was in the next room and she said I was actually performing the lines of dialogue, and I wasn't aware of that.

I used to get the total immersion feeling by writing at midnight. The day is not structured to write, and so I unplug the phones. I pull down the blinds. I put my headset on and play the same soundtrack of twenty songs over and over and I don't hear them. It shuts everything else out. So I don't hear myself as I'm writing and laughing and talking to myself. I'm not even aware I'm making noise. I'm having a physical reaction to a very engaging experience. It is *not* a detached process.

When I'm working on a book, I'm in a very agitated mental state. My sleep is disrupted. I only dream about the project. My sex drive goes up. My need for exercise, and the catharsis I get from exercise, is greater. When I'm in the middle of a project, whether I'm doing Bikram yoga or hiking up the hill or working out at the gym, I carry a blank pad and a pen. I'll take eight hundred little notes right in the middle of a posture. It drives my yoga instructor crazy.

Even if I'm trying not to think about it, I think about it. I get into an agitated mental state. So I can't do it all the time. You read these biographies of novelists, like John Updike, who get up early every single morning and write six hundred words. That's just not me. It would kill me to do that.

I'm mentally absent for months at a time. The social cost to my wife and kids is very high. Luckily, I'm a binge writer. I take a lot of time off between books, which is why I still have a family.

I get told all the time that I make writing a book look easy. I think my readers would be surprised to know just how agonizing it is, how sweat-intensive, how messy, how many drafts I write, how much doubt I have about the quality of prose. It might deter them from wanting to be writers.

Binge. Rest. Repeat.

Those piles on the windowsill? Each one is a project, a gathering storm. Right now those piles represent two magazine pieces, a screenplay, and three books. That may be the next five years of my life. Something could jump in and assert itself into those piles, but they're all real projects.

At any given time I usually have eight new ideas. But when the book is done, do I want to go do one of those ideas? No. So the eight ideas get pushed into one of those piles. I need time between projects. It's like a tank filling up. I can't just go from one to the other.

There's some cheating. Some books are just collections of magazine pieces, that kind of thing. It's never that I have writer's block; it's more that I lack the energy for the project, because the energy required is so great. And I know that the social cost to the family is pretty high. I'm here, but I'm mentally not here. I check out and check in.

When you have three kids in three different schools, you have no day. Right now it's softball season. I coach the two girls five days a week, two and a half hours each afternoon. There's not much left. You have a small window in which to write.

But it's nice to have those periods. It's nice to have the flexibility to say, I won't write much right now, but later I'll hit the gas. That's a function of money.

Money changes everything

Commercial success makes writing books a lot easier to do, and it also creates pressure to be more of a commercial success. If you sold a million books once, your publisher really, really thinks you might sell a million books again. And they really want you to do it.

That dynamic has the possibility of constraining the imagination. There are invisible pressures. There's a huge incentive to write about things that you know will sell. But I don't find myself thinking, "I can't write about that because it won't sell." It's such a pain in the ass to write a book, I can't imagine writing one if I'm not interested in the subject.

The first time was the best time

The high point of my life as a writer was seeing my first book when it actually physically arrived. As it happened, I was living next door to Judi Dench in London at the time, and she told me, "When your book comes, just drop it on the floor and listen to the sound it makes." I did that, and it was just *great*.

The best moment I'd had up until that point was when I knew the first book was working. When I heard the tumbler in the lock, like cracking a safe. I remember exactly where I was. It was eleven o'clock at night, and I was in the New York City subway, having just come from a dinner with a Salomon Brothers broker, when I realized how it was all going to fit together. It was going to be my story, the story of the markets. Oh my God! I thought, this is going to be fantastic. I had the fish on the hook. I saw how big it was. The only way I'd lose it would be to screw it up.

Those are the best moments, when I've got the whale on the line, when I see exactly what it is I've got to do.

After that moment there's always misery. It never goes quite like you think, but that moment is a touchstone, a place to come back to. It gives you a kind of compass to guide you through the story.

That feeling has never done me wrong. Sometimes you don't understand the misery it will lead to, but it's always been right to feel it. And it's a great feeling.

Michael Lewis's Wisdom for Writers

- It's always good to have a motive to get you in the chair. If your motive is money, find another one.

- I took my biggest risk when I walked away from a lucrative job at age twenty-seven to be a writer. I'm glad

I was too young to realize what a dumb decision it seemed to be, because it was the right decision for me.

- A lot of my best decisions were made in a state of self-delusion. When you're trying to create a career as a writer, a little delusional thinking goes a long way.

CHAPTER TWELVE

Armistead Maupin

There should be a rabbit hole *was what she was thinking.*
There should be something about this hillside, some lingering
sense memory—the view of Alcatraz, say, or the foghorns or
the mossy smell of the planks beneath her feet—that would lead
her back to her lost wonderland. Everything around her was
familiar but somehow foreign to her own experience . . .

—Opening lines, *Mary Ann in Autumn*, 2011

B ack in the literary stone age (pre-1980s), any writer who
happened to be gay was a "gay writer," and few gay writers
were published by mainstream houses since it was widely believed
that only gay readers would buy a "gay book." And so there were
gay publishers whose books were sold in gay bookstores, along
with gay newspapers, gay calendars, gay records, and gay gifts.

Many factors contributed to the changes that have trans-
pired since then, but a major one can be summarized in these
two words: Armistead Maupin. In 1976, when Gerald Ford was
president, a postage stamp cost thirteen cents, and *A Chorus
Line* won the Pulitzer for drama, Maupin launched a serial in
the *San Francisco Chronicle* called "Tales of the City," featuring

real, live gay people living alongside real, live heterosexuals. Ground was broken.

Maupin hasn't just made equal-rights history; he's participated in it. He married his true love, Christopher Turner, in San Francisco, mere weeks before Proposition 8 made same-sex marriage illegal again. Until their recent move to Santa Fe, the two shared an elegant, cozy, quintessentially San Francisco hillside home where they offered those in their social circle large doses of Southern hospitality.

THE VITALS

Birthday: May 13, 1944

Born and raised: Born in Washington, DC; raised in Raleigh, North Carolina

Current home: Temporarily itinerant

Love life: Married to Christopher Turner since October 4, 2008

Schooling: University of North Carolina at Chapel Hill

Day job?: No

Honors and awards (partial listing): Peabody Award, 1995; GLAAD Media Award, 1995; Publishing Triangle's Bill Whitehead Award for Lifetime Achievement, 1997; Trevor Project's Trevor Life Award "for his efforts in saving young lives," 2002; winner of the Big Gay Read (Britain's favorite gay-themed book), 2006; Litquake's Barbary Coast Award (first recipient) for literary contribution to San Francisco, 2007

Notable notes:

- Raised in a conservative North Carolina family, Maupin once regarded Jesse Helms as a "hero figure." He later con-

demned Helms in a speech on the capitol steps at Raleigh's
first gay pride parade.
- Maupin served several tours of duty in the U.S. Navy, including one in Vietnam during the war.
- *Tales of the City* has been translated into a dozen languages,
with more than 6 million copies in print. It's been made
into three television miniseries and a stage musical.

Website: www.armisteadmaupin.com

Facebook: www.facebook.com/armisteadmaupin

Twitter: @armisteadmaupin

THE COLLECTED WORKS

Novels

Tales of the City, 1978

More Tales of the City,
1980

Further Tales of the City,
1982

Babycakes, 1984

Significant Others, 1987

Sure of You, 1989

Maybe the Moon, 1992

The Night Listener, 2000

Michael Tolliver Lives,
2007

Mary Ann in Autumn,
2010

TV Miniseries

Tales of the City, 1993

More Tales of the City,
1998

Further Tales of the City,
1998

Film Adaptation

The Night Listener, 2006

Musical

Tales of the City, 2011

Armistead Maupin

Why I write

I write to explain myself to myself. It's a way of processing my disasters, sorting out the messiness of life to lend symmetry and meaning to it.

A dozen or so years ago, in *The Night Listener*, I wrote about a breakup while still going through it, believing this might lead to enlightenment. But I wasn't so much confronting my pain as containing it, stuffing it into a tidy in-box called "novel" that would keep the worst pain at a distance. Most writers channel their experience like this, but it's a tricky business. Life has to be something more than Material. The novel can end up writing you.

Sometimes I write to explain myself to others. Thirty-four years ago I told my folks I was gay through the *Tales of the City* character Michael Tolliver. They were following my *Chronicle* serial, so I used the shield of fiction to break the news to them. When Michael came out in a letter to his parents, my own parents were the ones who got the message. Writing gave me a way to frame my thoughts and feelings without the danger of actual confrontation.

Long before I started writing, I enjoyed telling stories and holding the attention of an audience. Southerners tend to do that. By the time I was eight I was putting folk legends and ghost stories into my own words, telling them around the campfire at summer camp and on Boy Scout trips. I was lousy at sports, but I could keep the other kids on the edge of their logs. I think I learned to find my self-worth that way.

Writing is not fun for me. The early part is fun—the perco-lating, as I think of it—but the actual process is glacial and full of self-doubt. I think of it as laying mosaic on my hands and knees, pushing the bits of color into place, knowing that the finished product is a long way from completion. I've learned to be disciplined about this only because of the pleasure that will come at the end. I'll get to stand in a room somewhere—last year in the big hall of the Sydney Opera House!—and read the words I've agonized over and be rewarded by the laughter and attentive silence of other people. We're on that log around the campfire again.

I don't mean to say that I don't have those glorious mo-ments when I look at a paragraph and find it every bit as grace-ful and illuminating as I wanted it to be. I've been known to do a little jig around the room when that happens. The problem is, I can't let myself proceed until I'm thoroughly happy with that paragraph. Every writer's manual on the planet tells you to just spill it all out and polish it later. I haven't been able to do that since the late seventies, when I was writing the serial on carbon paper, choosing my words and moving on immediately because of the daily newspaper deadline. The word processor, as much as I can't imagine life without it, has only made me pokier, since it enables me to polish endlessly. At best, I'll write only a page or two a day when working on a novel. I want my books to read like a brisk run through the woods, so my job is to get the obstacles out of the way. That takes time and sweat. A lot of people assume that a fast read is a fast write. Oh, if only that were true.

Somerset Maugham once said that he made three demands of his writing: lucidity, simplicity, and euphony. That pretty well describes my own goals, though euphony would probably come first for me. I think of it as finding the music.

Here's another reason I write: I'm still paying the mortgage on my house

Some people assume that famous writers are rich. I know a number who are quite comfortable, but most are still hustling to pay for necessities like everybody else.

I've designed the life I've wanted for myself, complete with home and husband, but it doesn't involve opulence. I've written ten novels over thirty-five years, which has allowed for some lovely leisure—a dividend in itself—and saved me from nine-to-five slavery under fluorescent lights. And here's what made it even sweeter: the thing I'd once feared most in myself—my homosexuality—became the very foundation of my success. I trusted my gut in this regard. There were plenty of folks in publishing three decades ago who advised me to cool it with the gay stuff. The closet was still very much entrenched, and my new-found openness was seen as an embarrassment—a professional liability, even. My mother once told me she was happy that I'd found myself, but she didn't want it to hurt my career. "You don't understand," I replied. "It *is* my career."

Being an openly gay artist was a rarified club in those days, so it brought some wonderful people my way. Christopher Isherwood and Don Bachardy became friends and guides. David Hockney asked me to sit for him. Ian McKellen sought my advice before he himself came out. There was also enormous satisfaction to be found in the readers who told me that *Tales of the City* had changed their lives—or at least helped them to see the beauty and nobility of their lives. I think I was able to do that because I wrote about everyone—gay, straight, and traveling—and presented them all as equally worthy and interesting.

Thank you, Mrs. Peacock

Mrs. Peacock was my senior English teacher in high school. She was a fey little bird of a woman who showed blatant favoritism toward students she thought to be talented. In the course of three or four years, she taught and singled out Anne Tyler, Reynolds Price, and me—all of whom sang her praises to the press after her death.

My senior English project was to create a staged presentation in the school auditorium that focused on some aspect of literature. I chose "sleep." I dressed all in white and performed next to a Doric column that I'd made out of ice cream cartons and Con-Tact paper. I read the "ravell'd sleeve" bit from *Macbeth* and concluded with Tennyson's "The Lotos-Eaters," a poem that is said to work as a soporific. Mrs. Peacock, bless her heart, demonstrated this feature by pretending to be asleep after the presentation.

It was a long, slow journey to a writing career after that. I wrote a satiric column for the *Daily Tar Heel*, the student paper at the University of North Carolina. I fancied myself as a cross between Art Buchwald and William F. Buckley Jr. I was the campus conservative, much to the pride of my father. I had to find some way to make my parents profoundly happy with me, because I knew there was something profoundly off about me that wasn't going to sit well.

From there I stumbled along on a disastrous course toward

the law. My father was a lawyer, and I'd been programmed to work in his law firm. I became the president of my Chapel Hill law class and proceeded to hang out at Fellini films in the downtown theater while my classmates were studying. Finally, at the end of my first year, I faced the truth. Not only didn't I want to spend the next two years in law school, I didn't want to spend the rest of my life being a lawyer. So I ended my law career at age twenty-two by walking out of my equity exam.

Oops—there was a war on

I went home to Raleigh and told my father I didn't want to be a lawyer. But this was 1967, the height of the Vietnam War, and being a student was my only possible draft exemption. With the help of Jesse Helms and a few of my father's cronies, I got assigned to officer candidate school. I served one tour of duty in Charleston and the Mediterranean, and a second tour in Vietnam.

When I got back from Vietnam, I moved back to Charleston. I spent a year working for the *News & Courier*, the South's oldest daily newspaper. I was writing feature stories about the Spanish moss blight and chitlin' festivals, interviewing Strom Thurmond and his third beauty queen wife. I started picking up guys down at the Battery, where the first shots of the Civil War were fired. Kind of appropriate, really, for the great-great-grandson of a Confederate general.

My sexual awakening—make that unleashing—was transformative. It made me question everything. Not just my sexuality, but my racism, my misogyny, all the bullshit I'd been raised with in Raleigh. I got restless fast in Charleston, so I interviewed with the Associated Press in New York. They offered me a job in Buffalo. When I rejected it, they offered me San Francisco.

San Francisco, here I come

I adored San Francisco, but I hated working for the AP. Wire service work means you're always on deadline. And I was always trying to make the stories more vivid, so I was very, very slow.

One of my bosses was quite mean about this one night when we were working together. "I'm on to you," he said, pointing his finger at me. "You're no reporter." I was a wreck for the rest of the evening, thinking I'd blown it as a writer. Last year this man waited in line to get my autograph at a book signing. I'm sure he didn't remember the time he'd trashed me, but I did.

I quit the AP after five months and looked for work elsewhere. I became a Kelly Girl, unloading mannequins from warehouses, handing out flyers. What agonizing shit that was. Then I worked as a mail boy and eventually as a copywriter at an ad agency, which gave me the color I needed to describe Halcyon Communications in *Tales of the City*. I hated that job, too. When I quit, I felt I should offer some excuse beyond sheer boredom, so I confessed to my boss that I was gay. He said, "So what? I'm fucking the secretary, and we're both married."

My big break came when I started doing a column about goings-on around town for the San Francisco edition of the *Pacific Sun*. I went to a nude encounter parlor. I wrote about Sally Rand, the seventy-year-old fan dancer. One day I checked out the hetero cruising scene at the Marina Safeway, where the girls were all dressed to the nines in their brushed denim pantsuits.

None of them would fess up to their reason for being there, so that night I went home and made up a new girl in town named Mary Ann Singleton. That's how *Tales of the City* was born.

Lucky me

I've had a unique opportunity with *Tales*. Interrupted by a few pleasant breaks for film work and other novels, I've been telling the same story for thirty-four years. Even my departure novels, like *Maybe the Moon*, have contained minor characters from the *Tales* universe. I've followed the same people through everything: love, death, marriage, birth, disease, self-discovery—the full catastrophe, as Zorba called it. It's like having a big yeasty ball of sourdough in the back room that's always there for me to draw on.

People sometimes ask if I know what my characters are up to at any given moment. No, of course not. But I know how to find them again. I just tap into whatever aspect of my own personality helped me identify them in the first place. In this way they become a scrapbook of my emotional terrain. The closer you get to your own raw nerves, the more likely you are to reel someone who feels the same way. And you get credit, of course, for being deeply candid and honest—even though, as any writer knows, there's always a certain amount of vanity involved in the boldest confession.

Armistead Maupin's Wisdom for Writers

- When embarking on your career, don't make all other writers your competition. What you create, if it's any good, will be yours and yours alone.

- Remember to play when you're working. It's easy to get lost in the drudgery, but good things can happen when you're being silly. Does that mean smoking a joint sometimes? For me it does.

- Writers' conferences are festivals of envy and contempt—dangling nerve ends all over the place. Stay away from them. The same goes for panels.

CHAPTER THIRTEEN

Terry McMillan

"Are you sure you don't want to come to Vegas with me?" my husband asks for the second time this morning. I don't want to go, for two reasons. First of all, it's not like he's inviting me for a hot and heavy weekend where I'll get to wear something snazzy and we'll see a show and casino-hop and stay up late and make love and sleep in and order room service. . . .

—Opening lines, *Getting to Happy*, 2010

"I write because the world is an imperfect place, and we behave in an imperfect manner . . . ," Terry McMillan told the *Writer* magazine in 2001. "Writing is about the only way (besides praying) that allows me to be compassionate toward folks who, in real life, I'm probably not that sympathetic toward."

By exposing the realities of African American women's lives to mainstream (which is to say, white) readers, Terry McMillan has written books that foster the compassion she seeks. Her 1992 novel, *Waiting to Exhale*, sold more than seven hundred thousand hardcover copies in its first year. By the time the movie version appeared in 1995, it had sold 2.5 million copies in paperback, thereby transforming the way the publishing industry thought about African American fiction. By kicking open the door that had been shut to African American writers, Terry McMillan proved that black women would buy books, if only they were offered books that reflected their real lives.

THE VITALS

Birthday: October 18, 1951

Born and raised: Port Huron, Michigan

Current home: Northern California

Love life: Single

Family life: Son, Solomon Welch, born 1984

Schooling: BA in journalism at UC Berkeley; studied screen-writing at Columbia

Teaching: University of Arizona; University of Wyoming; Stanford University

Day job?: No

Honors and awards (partial listing): Fellowships from the National Endowment for the Arts, New York Foundation for the Arts, and Doubleday/Columbia University; Before Columbus Foundation American Book Award, 1987

Notable notes:

- Terry McMillan first fell in love with books at age 16, when she worked in the Port Huron Public Library.
- McMillan is an avid art collector. She bought her first signed lithograph, now valued at $200,000, for $90 at age 22.
- McMillan never, ever reads her reviews. "You have a baby; do you really care if other people think it's cute?"

Website: www.terrymcmillan.com

Twitter: @msterrymcmillan

THE COLLECTED WORKS

Novels

Mama, 1987

Disappearing Acts, 1989

Waiting to Exhale, 1992

How Stella Got Her Groove Back, 1996

A Day Late and a Dollar Short, 2000

The Interruption of Everything, 2005

Getting to Happy, 2010

Nonfiction

Breaking Ice: An Anthology of Contemporary African American Fiction, 1990

It's Okay if You're Clueless, 2006

Film Adaptations

Waiting to Exhale, 1995

How Stella Got Her Groove Back, 1998

Disappearing Acts, 2000

Terry McMillan

Why I write

I didn't choose to write. It was something that just happened to me.

I write to shed dead skin and to explore why people do the things that we do to each other and to ourselves.

Writing feels like being in love. I am consumed by the characters I'm writing about. I become them. I lose all sense of my own reality when I'm writing a novel. It's refreshing, like running a few miles, the way you feel when you finish.

I don't write about stupid people. I don't write about victims. I write about people who are victimized, but they're not going to stay down. That said, I deliberately choose characters I'm not quite sympathetic toward, or that I truly do not understand.

Years ago I went to McDonald's and got an employment application. For every character I create, I fill one out. I use an astrology book to pick their birthdays based on the characteristics I want them to have. I create a five-page profile for every one of my characters so I know everything about them: what size shoes they wear, if their hair is dyed, if they bounce checks, have allergies, what they hate about themselves, what they wish they could change, if they pay their bills on time.

My readers might be surprised to know how much research I do. The novel I'm writing now is about grandparents becoming parents. I'm reading all kinds of books on that topic. I'm interviewing people who work for all these government agencies. When people read it, they won't know what went into it. They'll think it rolled off my tongue.

A novel is like life: it's a series of knots, and the quality of your life is determined by how you unravel them. I give my characters something to tackle. I let them tell me what the biggest challenge they're facing is, what they're most afraid of, and I make them face that challenge in my story. It's made me a more compassionate person. I start out not liking my characters and I end up caring for them. I have to step out of my own comfort zone to tell their stories.

I cry a lot when I write. In *Day Late*, when my character's mother died—oh my God, I was *messed up*. She'd left a purse in her closet with letters to her kids in it. When I was writing those letters I was a wreck. I got so many fan letters about those letters, saying they'd always wanted to get a letter like that from their mom.

I jump up in the morning. I can't wait to go see what my characters are going to do today. I get wired up. When my character falls in love, I'm in love. When somebody's heart is broken, or feels jubilation, I feel all of that. When I finish working for the day, I'm spent. I go for a walk or go do my errands, and I walk into the grocery store and it's like everything is illuminated. Nobody knows where I just came from. Nobody knows that I just left New York or Las Vegas. It's like I just walked out of one movie and into another one.

How it happened

When I was eighteen I was taking night classes at a junior college in L.A. I broke up with this guy and as a result, I wrote a poem. I wrote it on a steno pad, because I was this little stenographer for the Prudential Insurance Company during the day. Writing that poem kind of scared me. It was like I was possessed. I'd never written a poem in my life. I don't even remember *reading* a poem before then.

One afternoon, a friend of my roommate's read my poem. He wanted to know if he could publish it in the LACC (Los Angeles City College) literary journal. I said, *"Publish it?"* And he did. From that day forward, if a leaf fell off of a tree, I thought, There's a poem in that. I was just a little poem-writing fool.

I ended up going to UC Berkeley, majoring in sociology. I wanted to be a social worker because I knew the world was a horrible place, and I thought maybe I could help. Back then, if you were, like, a little Negro, they gave you money to go to Berkeley. Anyway, we started a black newspaper called *Black*

Thoughts, and they published some of my poems. I was writing editorials for the *Daily Californian* as well.

Word got around, and other university newspapers, especially the black ones, started publishing my poems. To this day I still have those poems in the cardboard suitcase I bought for two dollars and ninety-nine cents in Port Huron, Michigan, in 1968. And you know what? Some of them aren't really that bad!

In my junior year, when it came time for me to declare a major, I told my adviser I was declaring sociology. He asked me why; he said, "I've been reading your articles, and I can't understand why you're not focusing on writing."

My mouth fell open. I could not believe it. This guy was not black, either. I explained to him that writing was a hobby, that you can't make a living at it. He told me to go home and think about it, so I did. I realized he was right, so I switched my major.

I took a fiction writing class from Ishmael Reed. Ishmael read my first short story and he said, "Terry, you have a very strong voice." People were always saying I had an unusually deep voice for a woman, so I thought that's what he meant. I didn't know *anything* back then. Nada.

After Berkeley I moved to New York, and I got into the Harlem Writers Guild—kind of like the Iowa Writers' Workshop, but for black folks. I read them a story I'd written in Ishmael's class, called "Mama Take Another Step."

When I finished, this novelist, Doris Jean Austin, said, "This is not a short story, sweetie. It's a novel." Everyone was nodding. I didn't know there was no market for short stories, but they did. By the end of that session, I'd written the opening chapter of my very first book, *Mama*.

My life changed, and I didn't like it

In 1987, I got a seventy-five-hundred-dollar advance for *Mama*, and it sold out of its first printing before it hit the bookstores. I got seventy-five thousand dollars for *Disappearing Acts*. Those two didn't get on the *New York Times* list, but they sold a lot of copies. So I got a quarter of a million dollars for *Waiting to Exhale*.

In 1992, *Waiting to Exhale* debuted at number six on the *New York Times* list. I couldn't believe it. While I was on my sixteen-city tour for *Exhale*, my agent held an auction for the paperback rights. I was in Atlanta when my agent called me. She said, "Terry, you won't believe this. It's up to one point two." I was, like, "One point two *what?*"

A half hour later she called back and said, "Oprah wants you on her show." Oprah had never had a book author before. From that point forward a lot of things changed very quickly. I moved from Arizona to the Bay Area. From *People* magazine on down, everybody wanted interviews. I looked up and there was *Time* magazine, sitting in my living room. It was overwhelming.

Then this whole business that *black people do read* started coming to the fore. I resented that. I said, Black people have always read. There just hasn't been a contemporary novel that appealed to us in such high numbers. But guess what: there are a lot of white people buying my book. And guess what else: we've been reading a lot of books by white authors. Do the damn math.

When all this first happened, my life changed completely. I didn't like it. People started coming at me from every angle, asking for money. Readers wrote me their sad stories. I had long-lost relatives suddenly appear. I got so depressed, I went to see a shrink.

It didn't change things for just me

It didn't change my writing to be successful. I still told the stories that I wanted to tell. The thing is, the critics hate you when you become commercially successful. They look for stuff to find wrong. When I was writing *Getting to Happy*, I knew the book was not going to be well received. I didn't care. If the people reading the book like it, if it moves them, that's what matters to me.

But when all the hoopla happened after *Waiting to Exhale*, the publishers started giving lots of young black writers mega advances, thinking they could get themselves the next Terry McMillan. For a minute there, a lot of these writers were being paid these big advances. They were signing these two- and three-book deals for all this money, and they didn't understand that if your first book does okay, your second does mediocre, you're not going on tour for your third book. They didn't realize that if the publisher isn't recouping its investment, you're history.

When their books didn't sell the way *Waiting to Exhale* did, when they didn't earn back those advances, the publishers started punishing them by not giving them new contracts. Some of them had million-dollar deals. Now they've been kicked to the curb. They can't get a contract to save their lives. I know a lot of them. It's really sad. Really sad.

Racist, simple as that

There are a lot of white writers who get decent advances, and sell a decent amount of books, and they just keep going. Their publishers are willing to support them, regardless. They're going to promote them anyway. These writers run around the country, getting big speaking fees. You don't have a lot of black writers doing that. It's racist, simple as that.

I know some black writers—Iyanla Vanzant, for one—who got a lot of money, and their books did well, but not the way the publishers expected them to. Never mind that the publisher didn't promote them, didn't send them on mega book tours, any of that. They were relying on *my* audience to run out and buy those other black writers' books.

It even affects me. I have seventy pages of a new novel, and I'm being told, "It seems a little dark. It doesn't have your trademark humor in it."

I said, "Dark? Really?"

You know what? White people write depressing-ass books all the time. The more depressing it is, the deeper they think it is. Take *The Glass Castle*. Or Kathryn Stockett—she can write a book about black maids in the sixties. Talk about dark! What was so uplifting about that? And yet still it's been on the *New York Times* for a hundred weeks. But when we tell our *own* stories, it's either depressing or white people aren't interested.

The thing that pisses me off more than anything is that when writers, mostly white writers, use language that's so lofty, or they write about characters who would be inconsequential in real life, they make their characters' lives so important. Crossing the street is a big deal. What's in their cabinet is a big deal.

Take Jonathan Franzen. *Please.* After thirty pages, I was thinking, *Who cares?*

I hate labels of all kinds

The woman who came to my house for *Time* magazine spent more time talking about my house than she did on my books. She wouldn't have done that if I were a wealthy white writer. She was shocked that I have good taste.

In her article she described my books as "pop fiction." If your work is popular, that's a sign that you shouldn't be taken seriously. I wrote the magazine a scathing letter. I said, "Don't hate me because I happen to sell more books than your *Paris Review* little darlings. Don't try to make me the Wal-Mart writer. You know what? Popular is not a bad thing."

The way that I define "pop" is like pop psychology: you already know how it's going to end. My books are character driven, not plot driven. My books are not predictable. I mean, *Getting to Happy*—you don't know if they're going to get there. It's a journey. That's the whole point.

I'm doing basically the same thing that Chekhov, Virginia Woolf, Hemingway did. I'm telling stories about my world, in my time, in my own voice. No one held that against *them*.

In a hundred years they'll be able to eat those words "pop fiction." I reject them right now. I don't let anyone define me. I'm more interested in the story I have to tell. That's what's important to me.

So I'm going to keep on writing it the way I'm writing it.

Terry McMillan's Wisdom for Writers

- I only write about characters who disturb me. I don't sympathize with my characters at the beginning. In order to tell their story, I have to develop compassion for them by the end. That gives my characters, and me, *and* my readers an investment in how it all turns out.

- As soon as I understand what my characters' dilemmas are, I give them something to tackle, something they need to change, because people fear change more than anything and that makes for compelling drama.

- I don't put furniture polish on my stories and give my readers the shiny version. I tell it like it is.

CHAPTER FOURTEEN

Rick Moody

*People often ask me where I get my ideas. Or on one occasion
back in 2024 I was asked. This was at a reading in an old-
fashioned used-media outlet right here in town, the store called
Arachnids, Inc. The audience consisted of five intrepid and
stalwart folks, four out of the five no doubt intent on surfing
aimlessly at consoles.*

—Opening lines, introduction, *The Four Fingers of Death*, 2010

❝I have worked really hard to defy categorization, to break
down a taxonomy whenever it comes my way," Rick
Moody told an interviewer in 2002.

"Genre is a bookstore problem, not a literary problem. It
helps people know what section to browse, but I don't care about
that stuff. I'm trying to stay close to language first and foremost
and make sure that the paragraphs sing, that it sounds like music to me."

Indeed, since *The Ice Storm* was published in 1994, Moody's
books—not to mention his other artistic endeavors—would tax
any effort to taxonomize his work. Besides a writer of memoirs,
essays, novels, music criticism, story collections, novellas, and

combinations thereof, he's also a singer, guitarist, and piano player in a band, which he describes as "woebegone and slightly modernist folk music, of the very antique variety."

Born in New York City, Moody grew up in the Connecticut suburbs that have served as closely observed settings for many of his stories and novels. His reexaminations of the people and places of his youth included a critique of the Columbia University MFA program from which he'd graduated twenty years before. In a provocative 2005 *Atlantic Monthly* essay, he wrote, "What if all you did in class was *assignments*? What if you rewrote one sentence all semester? What if everyone got a chance to be the instructor, and everyone got a chance to be the student? Then, I think, we'd be getting somewhere."

THE VITALS

Birthday: October 18, 1961

Born and raised: Born in New York; raised in Connecticut suburbs

Current home: Brooklyn and Fishers Island

Love life: Married since 2002

Family life: Daughter born in 2008

Schooling: Brown University; MFA from Columbia University

Day job?: Teaches writing, part-time, at NYU

Honors and awards (partial listing): Guggenheim Fellowship; Addison M. Metcalf Award from the American Academy of Arts and Letters; PEN/Martha Albrand Award for Art of the Memoir; the *Paris Review*'s Aga Khan Prize

Notable notes:

- Rick Moody's grandfather was publisher of the *New York Daily News*.
- Moody is also a musician, composer, and music critic. He plays in a band called Wingdale Community Singers and writes a music column for TheRumpus.net.
- In 2006, an Arizona state senator advocated a measure allowing students to refuse "personally offensive" assignments—citing complaints he'd received about *The Ice Storm*.

Website: www.rickmoodybooks.com

THE COLLECTED WORKS

Novels

Garden State, 1992

The Ice Storm, 1994

Purple America, 1997

The Diviners, 2005

The Four Fingers of Death, 2010

Fiction Collections

Demonology, short stories, 2001

Right Livelihoods, novellas, 2007

The Ring of Brightest Angels Around Heaven, novella and short stories, 1995

Memoir

The Black Veil: A Memoir with Digressions, 2002

Film Adaptation

The Ice Storm, 1997

Rick Moody

Why I write

I abandoned two novels when I was in sixth grade. I got maybe
ten pages into each. One was about a kid who becomes vice
president. I still have the weird little blank book that I used
when I attempted to write it. The itch to do my job goes at least
that far back.

Why do I write? To do better for myself than I am capable
of doing with language, out there, in real time. To repair in-
abilities, to restore confidences. And, at this point, because I
don't know what else to do. I write just as I breathe and eat.
Every day. Habitually.

It would be easier if I could say that *one thing* happens when
I write, or, perhaps, a number of predictable things happen. But
the truth is that a great number of things have happened, over
the years, when I have been writing, and that these things are
unpredictable, hard to quantify, and mutable.

I guess I have now been writing, if I date my writing from
the first time I ever *rewrote* anything, for about thirty-three
years. Publishing books for about twenty. Sometimes the writing is inspired or inspiring; sometimes it is destitute of anything
but the need to keep working. I guess what I'm saying is that
what happens to me is so variable that it would be kind of fool-
ish to try to attach names to it. I do think, however, that just
about whenever I am writing, or more accurately, whenever I
have written, I feel better and more at peace as a human being.
That doesn't mean, unfortunately, that the literary product is
any good.

Responding to George Orwell's "four great motives for writing"

1. *Sheer egoism. "To be talked about, to be remembered after death, to get your own back on grown-ups in childhood, etc."*

   Writing out of bile, e.g., or out of some personal desire for gain—that just doesn't square with what makes literature useful, profound, etc. My reason is mainly neurotic, I suspect: I am never really comfortable *speaking*, and writing allows me the time and serenity to make better what I cannot do in speech. It's a peaceful and cloistered space, the page, where I don't feel pressured the way I do in the world.

2. *Aesthetic enthusiasm. "To take pleasure in the impact of one sound on another, in the firmness of good prose or the rhythm of a good story."*

   Yes, this is a possible reason to write. I imagine I am trying to think about prose the way I think about music. I try to think of prose as a musical form, not just as a code we agree to use in order to advance a plot. Aesthetic enthusiasm is mainly what motivates me, because aesthetic enthusiasm has no particular narrative requirements.

3. *Historical impulse. "The desire to see things as they are, to find out true facts and store them up for the use of posterity."*

   I sure hope posterity is interested in me, but I figure I'll be dead by then, and you can't take posterity with you when you are gone.

4. *Political purposes. "The opinion that art should have nothing to do with politics is itself a political attitude."*

A lovely sentence, really, and one I agree with. I think all art is political, but that some art, by being quiet about its politics, supports the status quo in a slightly sinister way. I have always tried to stake out political positions in what I do, but not in a manner, I hope, that is aesthetically dull (see number two), or too shrill, etc. I believe the two—aesthetics and politics—may go hand in hand. Even if that argument never sat well with the social realists nor with the art-for-art's-sake crowd.

Responding to Joan Didion

"Writing is the act of saying I, *of imposing oneself upon other people, of saying* listen to me, see it my way, change your mind.*"*

If it were just this, the first person, I would probably want to give up and do something else with my life. Although there's inevitability to "I," to a point of view that starts with self, it is not all there is. There is also "thou," as embodied in the reader. I see a real exchange with the reader, who is free to bring what she wants to the work. In this context, writing is not as expression of self, but as *relief* from self (T. S. Eliot, I believe).

Responding to Terry Tempest Williams

"I write to meet my ghosts."

Sounds interesting but might be too metaphorical and too hyperbolic for me.

Nomenclature

I am never terribly comfortable with the word *writer*.

I had a teacher, when young, who said the word *writer* was unimportant. He said that all that was important was the work itself. And I sort of agree with this approach. I think there's an instability that goes with writing, a lack of certainty, at least for me. This lack of certainty makes me more responsive to the world, more open to it. And so if I have to repel the word *writer* in order to maintain my openness and vulnerability to the world, then fine. I'll let go of the word. I do use it sometimes for the sake of simplicity, or so as to avoid confusing people, but I never feel totally comfortable about it.

First break

The first break I got was having my first novel published after sixteen months or so of failing to get anyone interested in it. Seemed like a big break to me at the time.

I always sort of thought I'd be a failure. I still sort of think I might be a failure. So just having a book out in the world made me very happy. I didn't much think, at first, about whether I was going to sell a lot of copies. I didn't pay attention to that sort of thing. I still don't. I don't think I have ever, not even once, willingly checked to see how many copies anything by me has sold.

In the years since my "big break," I have mainly made a living by writing, but also by teaching and doing campus workshops and appearances.

It's really hard for me to calve off the writing part from the just being alive part, and so I don't imagine I can really find a "best time" that just refers to my writing life. I think maybe the best thing that ever happened to me was becoming a father in 2008, although a close second would be checking myself into the psychiatric hospital in 1987. That turned out to be a very good move. I am a better writer for having fewer demons, and I am more curious about the world and the people in it. So those of you thinking you might need your demons in order to be creative: I beg to differ.

Hard time

Writing is always hard. As we all know, there's a lot of rejection involved.

Even now I find the rejection part of the job pretty challenging. I am not a strong enough person, in some ways, to live this life. I try not to envy other writers. I think nothing is worse for me, and for literature and the literary world. And don't even get me started on reviews.

I don't solve personal problems for myself by writing. The writing is the escape from the personal. Sometimes I *cause* problems, writing first and only thinking later. Those can only be solved in the usual ways, through time, conversation, willingness to reconcile, etc.

I think the good for me comes in continuing to work and trying, a little bit, to believe in what I do.

Caution: reading can lead to writing

I like books, the actual, physical things. I like to carry them around. I don't mind how heavy they are, and I don't need a lot of bells and whistles on my books.

Before I ever wrote, I was a voracious reader. Both my parents are people who always have a novel they're reading. A kind of object fetishism of book as a sacred object runs in my family and was imparted to me at a young age. I don't know exactly how long the book as we know it will exist, but I fully expect to make it to my death without having to give up on books.

Merciless

My big ambition is to avoid doing the same thing twice. The process of composition, messing around with paragraphs and trying to make really good prose, is an essential part of my personality, and I judge myself very, very harshly. I am all but entirely merciless about myself and my work. Alas. Those who are otherwise are probably healthier.

Rick Moody's Wisdom for Writers

- Trying to fit your writing into conventional commercial forms in hopes of getting published is a losing proposition. Losing more interesting experimental work to the constraints of the publishing industry would be a great loss for us all.

- Structure in a novel is something you discover, not something you superimpose. Don't sit at your keyboard and be a slave to an outline.

- When you're writing a novel, you have to keep the whole thing in your head. So it's good to go somewhere quiet to work, and it's good if you can find the time to binge on the work for a few days without interruption.

CHAPTER FIFTEEN

Walter Mosley

Somewhere beyond my line of sight a man groaned, pathetically.
It sounded as if he had reached the end of his reserves and was
now about to die.

But I couldn't stop to see what the problem was. I was too deep
into the rhythm of working the hard belly of the speed bag. That
air-filled leather bladder was hitting its suspension plate faster
than any basketball the NBA could imagine. . . .

—Opening lines, *When the Thrill Is Gone*, 2011

In the fine tradition of Raymond Chandler and Philip Marlowe—two of Walter Mosley's influences, along with Gabriel García Márquez, Langston Hughes, Dashiell Hammett, and Graham Greene—Mosley is inextricably linked to Easy Rawlins, the protagonist and namesake of his best-known mystery series. Some other associations: Bill Clinton. Blue Dress.

Not *Lewinsky's* blue dress, the one in the title of Mosley's first published book and first movie adaptation, *Devil in a Blue Dress*. As for the presidential connection, in 1992, candidate Bill Clinton famously called Mosley his favorite author.

At age sixty, nearly thirty years after he began writing, Mosley told me, "The fact that I ever got published is still amazing to me." Against all odds, maybe, but not amazing at all to anyone who has had the pleasure of reading his lightning prose.

THE VITALS

Birthday: January 12, 1952

Born and raised: Watts, Los Angeles, California

Current home: New York, New York

Love life: Divorced

Schooling: Victory Baptist Day School; Goddard College; graduated from Johnson State College, 1977; studied writing at City College of New York

Day job?: No

Honors and awards (partial listing): Anisfield-Wolf Award; Grammy Award; two NAACP Image Awards for Outstanding Literary Work—Fiction; Black Caucus of the American Library Association Literary Award; O. Henry Award; Sundance Institute's Risktaker Award; Carl Brandon Parallax Award; honorary doctorate from City College of New York

Notable notes:

- Mosley's mother was Polish Jewish; his father was African American.
- After high school Mosley spent time in Santa Cruz, California, and went to Europe; he dropped out of Goddard; and he began work toward a doctorate in political theory, then abandoned it.

- William Matthews, Edna O'Brien, and Frederic Tuten were Mosley's mentors.

Website: www.waltermosley.com

Facebook: www.facebook.com/waltermosleyauthor

THE COLLECTED WORKS

Easy Rawlins Mysteries

Devil in a Blue Dress, 1990

A Red Death, 1991

White Butterfly, 1992

Black Betty, 1994

A Little Yellow Dog, 1996

Gone Fishin', 1997

Bad Boy Brawly Brown, 2002

Six Easy Pieces, 2003

Little Scarlet, 2004

Cinnamon Kiss, 2005

Blonde Faith, 2007

Fearless Jones Mysteries

Fearless Jones, 2001

Fear Itself, 2003

Fear of the Dark, 2006

Leonid McGill Mysteries

The Long Fall, 2009

Known to Evil, 2010

When the Thrill Is Gone, 2011

All I Did Was Shoot My Man, 2012

Science Fiction

Blue Light, 1998

Futureland: Nine Stories of an Imminent World, 2001

The Wave, 2005

Socrates Fortlow Books

Always Outnumbered, Always Outgunned, 1997

Walkin' the Dog, 1999

The Right Mistake, 2008

Young Adult Novel

47, 2005

Other Novels

RL's Dream, 1995

The Man in My Basement, 2004

Fortunate Son, 2006

The Tempest Tales, 2008

The Last Days of Ptolemy Grey, 2010

Erotica

Killing Johnny Fry, 2006

Diablerie, 2007

Nonfiction

Workin' on the Chain Gang: Shaking Off the Dead Hand of History, 2000

What Next: A Memoir Toward World Peace, 2003

Life Out of Context, 2006

This Year You Write Your Novel, 2007

Twelve Steps Toward Political Revelation, 2011

Graphic Novel

Maximum Fantastic Four, 2005

Film and TV Adaptations

Devil in a Blue Dress, 1995

Fallen Angels, TV, 1995

Always Outnumbered, Always Outgunned, 1997

Play

The Fall of Heaven, 2010

Walter Mosley

Why I write

I really love putting words together to tell stories. It's a great thing to do. I can't think of a reason not to write. I guess one reason would be that nobody was buying my books. Come to think of it, that wouldn't stop me. I'd be writing anyway.

It's not like writing has been a lifelong thing for me. I've been drawing since I was little. I used to draw every day. But I only started writing in my thirties, and I fell in love with it. It's like a relationship. You meet someone, and suddenly you're in love when you didn't expect it. I could ask you why you're in love, but you wouldn't be able to tell me.

I like writing, but I don't fetishize it. If I write a sentence I really like, it's the same great feeling as when I do anything well: play an electronic game, play chess. There are more moments like that when I'm writing than when I'm doing anything else. But even when I'm just walking down the street, my life is a life of imagination.

Fire ants

Before I was a writer, I was a computer programmer. I didn't hate it, but there was no meaning to it. I didn't come home and imagine myself inside of my work, the way I do now.

One day I was at my job as a consulting programmer for Mobil Oil. It was on a weekend, so there was no one in the office. I was tired of writing programs, so I wrote this sentence: "On hot sticky days in southern Louisiana, the fire ants swarmed." I'd never been to Louisiana, and I'd never seen a fire ant, but I thought, "This sounds like the first line of a novel. Maybe I can write fiction." So I wrote my first book.

No one wanted to publish it. I couldn't even get an agent. The book isn't about white people or black women, and no one wanted to read about black men.

I thought I'd never get published. I decided I'd keep working, maybe take some classes to learn about writing, get a teaching job. After I'd been writing for about four years, I wrote *Devil in a Blue Dress* and gave it to a writer friend of mine. He gave it to his agent, and she said she'd like to represent it. She sold it within six weeks. Publishers were all looking for different kinds of mysteries. They thought a black mystery was a unique thing. It was a handle they could use to sell it.

The best moment of my career was getting my first book sold. It was so unexpected. I called my dad and said, "I sold a book. They paid me the same amount of money that I make in a year." He didn't believe it; I didn't, either.

That's how it all started. The book did okay, and people started paying attention to me. The best thing was I didn't have to work anymore, which was amazing.

Once I got started . . .

I couldn't stop. I didn't want to stop. I have three or four novels in my computer right now that nobody's bought. I haven't showed them to my agent. She says, "Not another book, Walter. I don't have time to read this book."

I had a collection of six novellas that I sent to her. She said, "Walter, I can't read this. I have other clients. I have four other books from you that I haven't had time to read!" I feel the same way I felt before my first book was published. I know they're good books. If you don't want to publish them, fine. Sooner or later someone's going to publish them.

Rejection can be sexy

The worst moment in a writer's life is the perpetual recurring moment, and that's rejection.

If you keep writing what you want to write, you're going to get a lot of rejection. "We're not printing this novel; it has too much sex in it." "We're not printing this nonfiction book; you're not a talking head. Who do you think you are?"

Rejection is always painful, but you learn to enjoy it. It's part of an incredible life, and you have to realize that you couldn't have this life without this pain. That pain becomes eroticized in a way. You kind of enjoy it. You love to get together with other writers and talk about the worst rejection you ever had.

I got a review in *Publishers Weekly* once: the guy said my characters weren't even strong cardboard. I love saying that to people. It's so funny. It's a terrible thing to say about any writer, even a writer who's in third grade, but hey, my book got published, so that's okay with me.

This is what I've decided to do. I'm like a boxer: getting hit is the worst moment and the best moment. I'm just trying to survive.

My problem

This sounds so crazy, but my biggest problem is capitalism. It works like this. People produce products on an assembly line, and then they're sold. If it's your job to put the front fender on the Pinto, you don't put the brakes in. You can't just decide to change what your job is.

Being a writer is the same. I write science fiction, nonfiction, books, TV shows, plays—I write everything. But people don't want me to write everything. It's the problem a lot of writers have. The more successful you are, the more problematic it's going to be. If you made a million dollars on one book, and now you write a book that's going to make only two hundred thousand, it's not just the publisher who starts to think the second book isn't as good. *You* start thinking it.

A lot of writers are defeated by the system of writing. I was talking to one recently. He said he couldn't get published, so he was thinking of quitting. I said, "You have to be kidding me, right? You're not writing for publication. You're writing to write." If you're looking to get married, you need another person. If you're looking to write, you really don't.

My favorite writers—Charles Dickens, Mark Twain—come from a time when publishing wasn't completely in the domain of capitalism. I'm a writer, not a seller. So I have to keep myself from thinking about the bottom line, so it's the publisher saying, "I want you to make a lot of money," not *me* saying it.

Genre ridiculousness

There's a hierarchy of writers in the publishing industry. There's so-called popular fiction, or commercial fiction, and then there's "literary fiction." People who like commercial fiction say, "Walter Mosley is a literary writer, so we don't have to pay attention to what he writes." The literary people say, "He's a popular writer, so we don't have to pay attention to him."

The terms are ridiculous. I don't care what you call me. The question is, is it a good book, or is it not a good book? Either one you want to do is fine with me. It takes a certain kind of talent to write a mystery, to imagine in that way.

Year after year I'm invited to host a table at literary awards ceremonies, but I've never been nominated. It's silly for me to be trying to raise money for you when your system of recognizing literature doesn't recognize me.

There's a whole group of "literary writers" who think they're the important writers and they hate "commercial writers." Well, guess what? There's not an important writer in history who wasn't a commercial writer. Shakespeare, Dickens, Twain, Dumas, Gogol, Dostoyevsky—every major writer in every genre was a popular writer. Melville's thing was writing adventures, but he was writing this deep stuff. He didn't tell people not to call them adventures. Melville wrote genre books, but he was a great, great writer. You don't have to categorize his books to love his books. That's the power of gorgeous writing.

If you write a nonfiction book about undocumented laborers in central California, the only people who are going to read it are people who already care about the issue. If you write a mystery about a Chicano with questionable papers who goes to kill the person who brought him across the border, you get all kinds of people reading that. People come to the genre because of something outside the story. But the story's still there. They'll get it.

I was talking to a "literary writer" one day. She said, rather proudly, "Not everybody can understand my fiction." I said, "That's not good. Your fiction should be accessible to everybody. As many people as possible should be able to read it and get something from it. If you wrote something that only ten people in the world can read, you didn't need to write that book."

What you need to do is have an even playing field where

you just talk about books: what do you think about this novel or short story? But nobody does that. In the end, what you can tell about the writing is in the writing itself.

The mysterious heart

Readers no longer need novelists to tell us what it's like to cross the world on a ship or fight a war. In the twenty-first century, we get that information in other ways. The thing that's still a mystery to us is the human heart. What we want is to understand people, what they're doing, and why they're doing it.

Walter Mosley's Wisdom for Writers

- The people who fail at writing are the people who give up because of external pressures, or because they didn't get published in a certain amount of time. You've got to exert your will over the situation.

- Writing is a long-term investment. If you stick with it, you'll reach the level of success that you need to.

- Don't expect to write a first draft like a book you read and loved. What you don't see when you read a published book is the twenty or thirty drafts that happened before it got published.

- Thomas Edison is not one of my favorite guys, but he said, "Genius is one percent inspiration, ninety-nine percent perspiration." He was right.

CHAPTER SIXTEEN

Susan Orlean

*He believed the dog was immortal. "There will always be a
Rin Tin Tin," Lee Duncan said, time and time again, to
reporters, to visitors, to fan magazines, to neighbors, to family,
to friends. At first this must have sounded absurd—just
wishful thinking about the creature that had eased his
loneliness and made him famous around the world. . . .*

—Opening lines, *Rin Tin Tin*, 2011

As a writer, what do you do and where do you go, once
Meryl Streep has been Oscar nominated for portraying
you in the movie adaptation of your book—or, in Susan Orleans's case, the movie, *Adaptation*, of her book? Susan Orlean
decided to do everything and go everywhere.

Susan Orlean is an exceptionally wide-ranging, voraciously
curious journalist with an exceptionally wide-ranging career. A
staff writer and blogger for the *New Yorker* since 1992, she's
written articles about nearly everything—chickens, dieting,
dogs, surfer girls, Jean Paul Gaultier, Bill Blass, a Harlem high
school basketball star, Tonya Harding, taxidermy—for *Rolling
Stone*, *Vogue*, *Esquire*, *Spy*, and a host of other publications.

"I always dreamed of being a writer," Orlean explains on her website, "but had no idea of how you went about being a writer—or at least the kind of writer I wanted to be: someone who wrote long stories about interesting things, rather than news stories about short-lived events."

A true American treasure, Orlean lives an adventure-filled writer's life. In doing so, she's created a definition of journalism that didn't exist before and remains unique to her. One suspects that if she were other-gendered, there would be a name for it, like Gonzo journalism or New Journalism. "Sue Journalism," perhaps.

THE VITALS

Birthday: October 31, 1955

Born and raised: Cleveland, Ohio

Home now: Columbia County, New York

Love life: Married since 2001 to CFO (and former *Harvard Lampoon* editor) John Gillespie

Family: Son, Austin, born 2004

Schooling: University of Michigan, Ann Arbor

Day job?: Staff writer for the *New Yorker* since 1992

Honors and awards (partial listing): Editor of *The Best American Essays 2005* and *The Best American Travel Writing 2007;* Nieman Fellow, Harvard University, 2003; Honorary Doctor of Humane Letters, University of Michigan, 2012

Notable notes:

- Susan Orlean was played by Meryl Streep in the film adaptation (*Adaptation*) of her book *The Orchid Thief.*

- The Hudson Valley home of Orlean and her husband and son is also home to nine chickens, three ducks, four guinea fowl, four turkeys, and ten Black Angus cattle.
- In 1998, Orlean wrote an article about surfer girls for *Women's Outside* magazine. In 2002 the article was made into the film *Blue Crush,* starring Kate Bosworth.

Website: www.susanorlean.com

Facebook: www.facebook.com/susan.orlean

Twitter: @susanorlean

THE COLLECTED WORKS

Nonfiction

Red Sox and Blue Fish, 1987

Saturday Night, 1990

The Orchid Thief, 1998

The Bullfighter Checks Her Makeup, 2001

My Kind of Place, 2004

Rin Tin Tin: The Life and the Legend, 2011

E-book

Animalish, Kindle Single, 2011

Film Adaptations

Adaptation, 2002

Blue Crush, 2002

Articles

Too numerous to list!

www.susanorlean.com /articles

Susan Orlean

Why I write

Writing is all I've ever done. I don't think of it as a profession. It's just who I am.

I write because I love learning about the world. I love telling stories, and I love the actual experience of making sentences. From age five or six, the earliest time I could imagine myself as a person with a job, being a writer was all I imagined I'd be. I'd fallen in love with the idea of stories—telling them and hearing them. I was enchanted. The only problem was that when it came time to leave college and have a profession, I thought, Jesus, how do you make it a job?

My parents wanted me to go to law school. I grudgingly proposed that I would, if they'd let me first take a year off after finishing college. During that year I managed—very unexpectedly—to land a job as a writer at a little magazine in Portland. I had gone to the interview for the job with no clips, no experience, but a lot of passion; in fact, I basically announced, "You just have to hire me. This is all I want to do. Just this." Frankly, hiring me was a very good decision for them, because wanting to be a writer is a huge percentage of what makes you be one. You have to want to do it really badly. You have to feel that's what you're supposed to be doing. That's how it was for me. From the moment I got that job, being a writer was utterly and totally a fit I'd never experienced anywhere else. I didn't have training. I learned on the job and from a series of very good editors. I think my pure desire made up for my complete lack of knowledge and experience.

True to my promise, one year later I took my law boards. But then I informed my parents that I wasn't going to law school. My father was furious with me. I think he was worried about it being a real gamble as a way to make a living. Even after my first book came out, he was still suggesting that it wasn't too late to go to law school as a fallback. I said, "Dad, I don't plan to fall back." If I'd had a fallback I might not have toughed this out and made it work.

A lot of my friends who thought about being writers ended up going into law or advertising or PR. They still dreamed about writing, but they couldn't give up their good jobs. Fortunately I never had a good job to give up.

All the work's a stage

When it comes to nonfiction, it's important to note the very significant difference between the two stages of the work. Stage one is reporting. Stage two is writing.

Reporting is like being the new kid in school. You're scrambling to learn something very quickly, being a detective, figuring out who the people are, dissecting the social structure of the community you're writing about. Emotionally, it puts you in the place that everybody dreads. You're the outsider. You can't give in to your natural impulse to run away from situations and people you don't know. You can't retreat to the familiar.

Writing is exactly the opposite. It's private. The energy of it is so intense and internal, it sometimes makes you feel like you're going to crumple. A lot of it happens invisibly. When you're sitting at your desk, it looks like you're just sitting there, doing nothing.

Writing gives me great feelings of pleasure. There's a marvelous sense of mastery that comes with writing a sentence that sounds exactly as you want it to. It's like trying to write a song, making tiny tweaks, reading it out loud, shifting things to make it sound a certain way. It's very physical. I get antsy. I jiggle my feet a lot, get up a lot, tap my fingers on the keyboard, check my e-mail. Sometimes it feels like digging out of a hole, but sometimes it feels like flying. When it's working and the rhythm's there, it does feel like magic to me.

Where I write

I don't need to be in a perfectly quiet place to write. I don't need a lot of fussy special conditions. But I do need the material that I work from within reach, and I do need a certain sense that I'm not going to be interrupted for a chunk of time.

That means I find it really hard to write when my son, Austin, is in the house. I can report in any situation, but writing—no. Austin used to ask if he could just sit in my studio while I wrote; he promised to be quiet. I thought, There's no way in a million years I can write with this little person there. No way he could be quiet, either.

After Austin was born, it became pretty important to have a private workspace, so I built myself a little studio. It's only fifty yards from the house, but it has a door I can close. I have a very Virginia Woolf need for my own space—not my old space, which was the dining room table. I don't need it to look a certain way; I just need to feel it's mine. I need to put things on the wall that don't require approval from anyone else. I need to be able to leave at night with my notes laid out in a certain way and know they'll be exactly that way when I return in the morning.

I got lucky

Unlike most postcollege first jobs, the first job I got out of college, at that magazine in Portland, Oregon, was an actual writing job, not being an assistant to a writer. My editor told me to think of ideas that would make good stories, and then he told me to go do them. When the magazine folded, I briefly worked at a radio station doing odds and ends, and then I got another writing job at the *Willamette Week*.

My first big break came in '79 or '80 when I was twenty-whatever. A senior editor at *Rolling Stone* who'd grown up in Portland saw my stuff in the *Willamette Week*. He called me and said, "You should be writing for *Rolling Stone*." I almost fell over. It opened the door for me. I started contributing to *Rolling Stone*, and then the *Village Voice*, and then I began figuring out ways to freelance for other national publications.

I'm surprised by how shrewd I was about how to make my way in the writing world. Portland wasn't exactly the hotbed of the writing world, but there were stories happening there, interesting stories. So I contacted national magazines and said, "I'm here, and I know some good stories here, so let me do them." For instance, Bhagwan Shree Rajneesh, a cult leader, had bought a huge, ten-thousand-acre ranch in Oregon and established a community of his followers there. He was a controversial figure who owned forty-eight Rolls-Royces while preaching anti-materialism, and yet many very intelligent, educated people had joined his group. It was a fascinating situation, so I contacted the *Village Voice* and said, "I'm here, and I'd love to write about it." They had nothing to lose since they didn't have to pay to send me out to Oregon, so they told me to go ahead. In the end, my piece ran as a cover story in the *Voice*, and through sheer luck the week it ran happened to be the very first time they used color on the cover, so the piece got lots of extra attention because of that. It was one of many instances when I felt I just had good fortune on my side.

I started getting calls after my story ran in the *Voice*, and I started writing for *Mademoiselle*, *Vogue*, and *GQ*. I was a new, young writer, not living in New York, so for many editors, I offered a wonderful sense of discovery, to find a new writer. I left Portland and moved to Boston. I started itching to move to New York, and in 1986, I finally did.

And then I got luckier

The best time I've ever had as a writer—this is strange, but true—was years ago when I was reporting a story for the *New Yorker*, and I traveled with a black gospel group for a couple of weeks, writing about their world.

There was this moment when we pulled into some tiny town in Georgia, and we were having dinner in a local diner and I had an out-of-body experience. I couldn't stop being amazed, thinking, This is my job. I'm in Georgia with this black gospel group, and I'm talking with people I would never have met as long as I lived if this wasn't my job.

I was feeling the exhilaration of stepping into an alternate universe. If my life had taken a different path, I might have been having dinner at a country club in a suburb in the Midwest, but I'm not. I'm here. I've had a version of that experience many times, and it's always so powerful.

And then it got hard

The hardest thing I've ever been through in my career was being several years late with *Rin Tin Tin*, and having a young child, and being confronted by my publisher asking where the book was, and feeling simply overwhelmed.

Frankly, that moment was one I'm not sure a lot of men would have experienced: *I can't do this all.* I don't know how to be a writer with the demands of having a kid. That was my hardest, lowest point ever as a writer. It's funny, because I'd like to say that my hardest time ever was struggling with a sentence. But that's the one situation that I thought would get the better of me.

I got the contract for *Rin Tin Tin* in January 2004, and I got pregnant that spring. It was a challenging book. I loved the idea but I didn't know how to write it. It was a book I had to wrestle into shape. Then Austin was born, and I realized I'd never figured out how I was going to go do the reporting I needed for the book with an infant to take care of. Time just started adding up.

Originally I'd asked for two years to write the book, which was ridiculous. I said I could do it that quickly because I was trying to make my publisher happy. They'd paid me a lot of money, and I wanted to make it sound as if they'd have their money back in no time at all; they'd hardly miss it. What I should have said was, "Give me eight years because I have no idea how long it's going to take."

Your publisher is a frenemy in the most pure sense. You

pretend you're on the same team but in many ways, you're not. You don't want them to see the slightest shred of weakness because you don't want them to begin to question the project or their belief in you. So instead of saying, "I don't have a fucking clue how to do this book; give me more time," you say, "It's a breeze; I can do it in my sleep." I wanted them to think I was just the easiest author on earth, that everything about this experience would be easy for them and profitable and fantastic.

I can't blame publishers; it's just a part of my personality. I want to please people. I feel like I should always be the good girl. I haven't developed a diva routine in which I say, "Hey, you should give me a lot of money and I get to be as difficult as I want to be."

The fact is that I got multiple extensions because *Rin Tin Tin* was proving to be much bigger, more complicated, and much harder to do because I couldn't travel hither and yon easily to do the research I needed to do. And I didn't feel I could reveal my vulnerability to my publisher.

I got two extensions for one year each, because I was wary about asking for a much, much longer extension, which was what I needed, because I thought it would indicate that I was having trouble. So then I was late, and then late again.

In a way it was the best thing that ever happened to me. When I asked for yet another extension, my publisher balked, and it became clear that they were no longer that invested in my book. So I got out of the contract and went to another publisher that really embraced the book and understood my need for more time. I took a loss on my advance, but I was philosophical about it. Advances are just that—advances. They're not payments. They're not awards.

It's a job—and an art form

It makes me cringe to call myself an artist. Even if it's true.

I'm making art of a kind. At the same time I'm very pragmatic. I don't treat myself as this precious flower. The fact that writing is a *job* doesn't undercut the fact that it's also an art.

When I was first getting started, I thought, What's important for me is to write as much as possible. If that means writing for fashion magazines, I'll do it, even if that isn't where I dreamed of writing, but I'll do a good job of it. I had friends who said, "Ew, you're writing for women's magazines? I'd never write for that magazine." I thought, How nice for you to be so picky. And anyway, I'm going to write a great piece wherever it runs.

I think the content is more important than the context. And I figured that if I wrote well, eventually I'd get to pick where I got published. I can write a really good story for *Vogue* or *Mademoiselle* or anywhere, and I can say with pride that it's not all about the packaging surrounding the story: my pride is about the story itself. That's a pretty practical attitude, and I'm glad I have it. It's served me well. That's my attitude about life, too.

Susan Orlean's Wisdom for Writers

- You have to simply love writing, and you have to remind yourself often that you love it.

- You should read as much as possible. That's the best way to learn how to write.

- You have to appreciate the spiritual component of having an opportunity to do something as wondrous as writing. You should be practical and smart and you should have a good agent and you should work really, really hard. But you should also be filled with awe and gratitude about this amazing way to be in the world.

- Don't be ashamed to use the thesaurus. I could spend all day reading *Roget's*! There's nothing better when you're in a hurry and you need the right word *right now*.

CHAPTER SEVENTEEN

Ann Patchett

The news of Anders Eckman's death came by way of Aerogram, a piece of bright blue airmail paper that served as both the stationery and, when folded over and sealed along the edges, the envelope. Who even knew they still made such things? This single sheet had traveled from Brazil to Minnesota to mark the passing of a man, a breath of tissue so insubstantial that only the stamp seemed to anchor it to this world. . . .

—Opening lines, *State of Wonder*, 2011

Whether she's stitching silver threads between an opera star, a businessman, and a band of terrorists; bringing a magician out of the deepest possible closet; or shining a bright light on race, class, and family, Ann Patchett is a master of the page. In her novels, in her searing 2004 memoir, and in the 2006 commencement address she delivered to her alma mater, Sarah Lawrence College—a speech that gathered so much notice, it grew into a book called *What Now?*—Patchett writes with pure poetry, and pure ferocity.

"'What now?' represents our excitement and our future," she wrote in that book, "the very vitality of life." The question represents the essence of Ann Patchett, the human being and the bestselling author as well.

THE VITALS

Birthday: December 2, 1963

Born and raised: Born in Los Angeles, California; raised in Nashville, Tennessee

Current home: Nashville, Tennessee

Love life: Married to Dr. Karl VanDevender

Schooling: Sarah Lawrence College; Iowa Writers' Workshop

Day job?: No

Honors and awards (partial listing): Janet Heidinger Kafka Prize; PEN/Faulkner Award; the Orange Prize; Book Sense Book of the Year; finalist for National Book Critics Circle Award

Notable notes:

- In November 2011, following the closure of two Nashville bookstores, Ann Patchett and her business partner, Karen Hayes, opened Parnassus Books.
- Patchett's parents divorced when she was six, and her mother moved her and her sister from L.A. to Nashville. She credits her start as a writer to her need to write letters to her adored dad.
- A confirmed homebody, Patchett once wrote, "Home is the stable window that opens out into the imagination."
- Patchett's closest friend is Elizabeth Gilbert, author of *Eat, Pray, Love.*

Website: www.annpatchett.com

THE COLLECTED WORKS

Novels

Taft, 1994

The Patron Saint of Liars, 1992

Bel Canto, 2001

The Magician's Assistant, 1997

Run, 2007

State of Wonder, 2011

Nonfiction

Truth & Beauty, 2004

What Now?, 2008

Ann Patchett

Why I write

I write because I swear to God I don't know how to do anything else.

From the time I was a little child, I knew that writing was going to be my life. I never wavered from it. Making that decision very young made my life streamlined. I put all my eggs in one basket, which has resulted in a great number of eggs.

I don't like to look back. That's a big part of my psychology. It's not because of lurking trauma. I don't particularly look forward, either. I'm all about the now. But writing gives my life a narrative structure: "Oh God, this happened and then I did that . . . I shouldn't have done that, but then I did this."

You know that old cliché, "I hate to write but I love to have written"? That pretty much sums it up. How I feel about writing depends entirely on what I'm working on. At the moment I'm writing an essay about marriage. It's excruciating. I feel like I'm sitting on the asphalt on a pitch-black interstate, typing madly, while the eighteen-wheelers are bearing down on me. Every minute, I'm about to be squashed.

Fiction is different, because in fiction you're just trying to find what happened. I always feel I'm squinting at something in a snowstorm very far away, trying so hard to make it out.

What if I didn't write? What would happen to me? I'd get to read all these books that are stacked up all over my office, that's what! I said to my husband last night: I really just want to take a month off and read.

I love to write. I think of it as a privilege and a pleasure. But if something happened and I never wrote again, I'd be fine. It would be a less interesting life—less dimensional—but it wouldn't be an unhappy life. I was given the gift of very good brain chemistry. I've had hard times in my life, but I've never had depression.

Luddite-ish

Can you believe it? I still write in WordPerfect. Why? Certainly not because I'm superstitious. I'm passionately against superstitions, talismans, ritual, routines. When you're a writer, it's so easy to become a freak.

Everything I have is in WordPerfect, and I can't bear to contemplate changing that. It's like being on a train: it's too late to get off fifteen stops ago. I just got an iPad. I haven't learned to use it yet, but the first thing I did was to download the WordPerfect app.

Nondesperate housewife

I think it might surprise my readers to know that I'm a house-wife in Nashville, and I've got a really dull life. People imagine that I live so glamorously. The truth is, I stay home as much as I possibly can. And when I am home, I do the laundry, I keep house. I'm like a dream wife because I make all this money and I make a really good dinner every night and everything's clean. I iron all the handkerchiefs. I'm extraordinarily lucky to have a happy, happy marriage.

People ask me, "If you could go anywhere you want to go, where would you be?" And I say, "Home." I don't go to artists' colonies to write now that I'm older. I want my work to be at home. I don't ever want to tell myself that I work better some-place else. I want to work the very best at home.

Fiction and nonfiction

I was a contributing editor at *Bridal Guide* for one year, and a freelance writer for years after that, starting when I was twenty-two. Since then I've had a very healthy career as a magazine writer and an essayist. I know what it means to write for money, to write for an audience. I just love writing essays, but I do a lot less of it now because there are fewer magazines. I enjoy it, but I'd never sit down and write an essay unless someone asks me to do it.

I figured out very early that I could make as much money writing magazine articles as I could teaching, and that maga-zine writing is infinitely easier. I'm a fiction writer. Do I want to spend three months writing a piece on global warming for the

Nation for seven hundred dollars or a piece on shoes for *Vogue* that takes three hours and pays me three thousand dollars? You don't have to ask me twice. I hardly ever say no to a magazine assignment. I'm a novelist, so it's fun to do something I'll be done with in one night. When I'm holed up for years at a time writing a novel, my friends can see my name in a magazine and know that I'm not dead.

Just last week I wrote a piece for a catalog that sells "tools for writers." They're doing a little book to sell in their catalog about writers and their talismans. They asked me to write eight hundred words, for which they'd give me a two-hundred-dollar gift card. I thought, turning them down will take more energy than writing it. So I wrote a piece about how much I like having my dog around while I write.

Nonfiction is totally different from fiction. If you're writing an eight-hundred-page book about Chihuahuas, you need to make sure that no one else will turn in their book about Chihuahuas before you do. That's not really a problem with a novel.

When I was halfway through *Truth & Beauty*, there were inklings that someone else might be writing about my friend Lucy Grealy. So I sold the book before it was finished, to make sure I had a publisher who was committed. But I was going to write that book whether a publisher bought it or not.

As far as fiction is concerned, I've never sold a book before I finished it and I never will. I write fiction entirely for myself. I write the book I want to read. It's the story in my head that I can't find in an existing book. The commercial success, or potential commercial success, of a book has no impact on me.

Let's remember: writing a book isn't curing cancer. This is

literary fiction. It doesn't add up to a hill of beans. If I write something terrible or weird, fine. If I turn in a book and my publisher says, "Ann, this is not for us," if I don't agree with their critique, I'll go to another publisher rather than make changes.

When I finished *Bel Canto*, an editor who read it said, "I like the book, but there are some things I'll take out. That Russian character is dreadful." I said, "I really respect your opinion. Good luck with your life." Thank God I didn't have a contract with that editor, so I didn't have to take the Russian out. I never want to feel like an indentured servant to a publisher.

Lucky

I say all the time that I had the last great writing career, because I was allowed to have it. I feel very, very fortunate that I got on board when I did.

I published my first book at twenty-seven, at a time when a publisher was willing to stick by their authors, even the ones who didn't sell a million copies. In my early days, if you looked up the definition of a midlist author, you'd find a picture of me. But I kept writing books, and they kept giving me advances. I got forty-five thousand dollars for *Patron Saint*, fifty thousand dollars for *Taft*, fifty-five thousand for *The Magician's Assistant*. Writing was my job, and my advances went up slowly and steadily, like getting raises at the office.

I don't know who gets forty-five thousand dollars for a first novel anymore. Everyone thinks Liz Gilbert had a huge hit with her first book, but *Eat, Pray, Love* was her fourth book! Before that she published a beautiful collection of short stories,

a novel, and a biography. No one realizes she wasn't an overnight success.

Nowadays, publishers look at your sales numbers, and if
you're not coming in with enough, you're through. I was lucky it
was my fourth book that was a big hit. The success didn't mess
with my mind the way it might have if I'd had that kind of hit
with my first.

Orange you glad?

My happiest moment as a writer was winning the Orange Prize,
in part because I'd lost it for *Magician's Assistant.* At the time
that I lost, I thought it was fine because it's such a pleasure to be
nominated, and because Carol Shields won, and she should
have won. But when I won I thought, "Oh my God, this is
really better. This is a lot more fun than losing."

My father, stepmother, husband, and my English cousins
came to London for the ceremony at the London Opera House.
It was such a glamorous night, really over-the-top gorgeous-
ness. My psychological makeup is such that it's very hard for me
to access the moment, especially a moment in which I'm winning. But I felt that moment and it felt great.

Happiness is a good hotel

As my books have started selling in large numbers, here's what's
changed in my career: I get better hotel rooms.

When I started, I drove my book tours. I had a budget. I
had to get to twenty-three cities for three thousand dollars. I
drove every night till I was falling asleep.

That's changed. I have the most amazing publicist. Say what you want about your editor and your agent, but it's your publicist who makes you or breaks you. My publicist has been with me from *Bel Canto*. Did my career get a whole lot better because my publicist got a whole lot better? That seems really likely.

When my last editor got a job at a different publishing house, she wanted me to come with her. I told her, "You know there's no way in the world I'd leave my publicist. You'll have to get her to switch houses, too." My publicist is the architect of my life. She'll call me and say, "They want you to do this thing in Wisconsin." I say, "If you want me to do it, I'll do it." There's nothing more important to me than my time, and she's in charge of my time.

I have a friend whose book is coming out soon. It's her first time with a new publishing house, and the publicist is abominable. I've been trying not to tell her, "You're sunk. If your publicist is this bad, it's over."

Truth and books

I'm a very truth-oriented person. I know that as I'm writing, I'm going to keep telling myself to tell the truth about everything. At the same time, I am such a good girl that I don't want to write things that might hurt or upset anyone. I wouldn't have written *Truth & Beauty* if Lucy hadn't died.

But now I'm pushing fifty. It's time to be able to write about anything I want to write about. I don't want to make allowances as I'm going along, trying to save this person or that person's feelings.

Anyway, the truth is such a subjective thing. While I was writing about Lucy, a friend of hers called and asked me how the book was coming along. I told her I was up to the part about Lucy getting breast implants. Her friend said, "That was a huge secret. Lucy didn't want anyone to know." I said, "What? Lucy was so proud of those breasts. She showed them to everyone."

So I called another friend and asked her what to do. She told me, "The first time I ever met Lucy, she had her shirt off. She was Xeroxing her breasts in the Radcliffe office." There you have it: different people, different truths.

Ann Patchett's Wisdom for Writers

- Don't be afraid to make money writing the kinds of things you'd never write for the fun of it. There's no shame in earning a living, and whatever you write, even catalog copy or fluffy magazine articles, makes you a better writer.

- Writing about my happy marriage is a lot more difficult, a lot more intimate, than writing about the unhappy stuff. But it's my story to tell, and if I think I can learn something important, or share something important, I'll tell it.

- Staying focused, sitting at your desk, is your number one job as a writer. There's always something else to do. Don't do it! Remember, time applied equals work completed.

CHAPTER EIGHTEEN

Jodi Picoult

One sunny, crisp Saturday in September when I was seven years old, I watched my father drop dead. I was playing with my favorite doll on the stone wall that bordered our driveway while he mowed the lawn. One minute he was mowing, and the next, he was facefirst in the grass as the mower propelled itself in slow motion down the hill of our backyard.

—Opening lines, *Sing You Home*, 2011

Jodi Picoult has published twenty novels in the past twenty years, the past six of them blockbuster bestsellers. Four of her books were made into Lifetime movies; one was made into a feature film. She's been a regular on the *New York Times* bestseller list ever since, and her books have sold more than fourteen million copies worldwide.

Picoult's novels have connected with her readers in a way that is every publisher's dream *and* every author's. From school shootings to organ donation to autism, her books have connected the hottest social issues of our time to the deepest, most universal emotional dilemmas.

With the 2011 publication of *Sing You Home*, Jodi Picoult

stepped out from behind the writerly curtain and became an eager advocate for gay rights—the issue at the core of the novel and at the core of her family, which includes her gay son. Picoult is active on Twitter, where her profile photo shows her with silver duct tape over her mouth, "NO H8" stenciled onto her cheek, and her fingers arched to form a heart.

THE VITALS

Birthday: May 19, 1966

Born and raised: Long Island, New York, and New Hampshire

Current home: Hanover, New Hampshire

Love life: Married to Tim Van Leer

Kids: Samantha, 16; Jake, 18; and Kyle, 20

Schooling: Graduated from Princeton University, 1987; master's in education from Harvard; honorary doctorates from the University of New Haven and Dartmouth

Day job?: No

Honors and awards (partial listing): New England Book Award for fiction; Alex Award; BookBrowse Diamond Award; Lifetime Achievement Award from Romance Writers of America; *Cosmo*'s Fun Fearless Fiction Award; Green Mountain Book Award; Virginia Readers' Choice Award

Notable notes:

- Picoult's first unpublished work was a story called "The Lobster Which Misunderstood." She wrote it at age five.
- Although Jodi Picoult is known as one of the bestselling American authors, it was her tenth book that first hit the bestseller list.

- Picoult wrote DC Comics' *Wonder Woman* series from March 28 to June 27, 2007.

Website: www.jodipicoult.com

Facebook: www.facebook.com/jodipicoult

Twitter: @jodipicoult

THE COLLECTED WORKS

Novels

Songs of the Humpback Whale, 1992

Harvesting the Heart, 1994

Picture Perfect, 1995

Mercy, 1996

The Pact, 1998

Keeping Faith, 1999

Plain Truth, 2000

Salem Falls, 2001

Perfect Match, 2002

Second Glance, 2003

My Sister's Keeper, 2004

Vanishing Acts, 2005

The Tenth Circle, 2006

Nineteen Minutes, 2007

Change of Heart, 2008

Handle with Care, 2009

House Rules, 2010

Sing You Home, 2011

Film and TV Adaptations

The Pact, 2002

Plain Truth, 2004

The Tenth Circle, 2008

My Sister's Keeper, 2009

Salem Falls, 2011

Jodi Picoult

Why I write

I write because I can't *not* write. Just ask my husband. If I have an idea circling in my brain and I can't get it out, it begins to poison my waking existence, until I'm unable to function in polite company or even hold a simple conversation.

When I'm actively writing, in the thick of a book, I'll find myself hiding up in my attic office to get just one more scene down on the page before I go downstairs to dinner. A lot of times, that one scene will turn into two or three.

But beyond the itchiness I'd feel if I weren't able to write, I write because it's a way of puzzling out answers to situations in the world that I don't understand. The act of writing a book gives me the same experience that I hope reading it gives readers. It forces me to sort through the various points of view on a given issue or situation and ultimately come to a conclusion. Doing that might not change my mind, but it almost always gives me a stronger sense of why my opinion is what it is—a question we rarely ask ourselves.

Riding a bike down a hill

The way I feel about writing changes on a daily—or an hourly—basis. Sometimes it's like riding a bicycle down a hill, with the wind whipping through my hair and my hands in the air. And then there are the times when writing feels like slogging through the mud that was left behind after Hurricane Irene.

I've always seen writing as a job. Granted, it's one I love to do, but it requires me to park my butt in a chair even when I don't feel particularly motivated.

Sometimes, it's magical. The characters seem to breathe and take over. I hear their voices very clearly in my head. That's why I've always called writing "successful schizophrenia": I get paid to hear those voices. But at a certain point in every book, *something* happens that I never saw coming—at least, not consciously—and it's exactly the puzzle piece the story is missing, the element that ties the threads of the book together. Characters seem to pick their own paths. They have an agenda that I don't even know about until the conversation or the plot begins inching its way across the typed page. Even though I know the end of my books before writing a single word, I often find that the middle section—how I get from point A to point Z—is a delightful surprise.

I'm often asked if I cry when I write. Of course I do! There are some scenes I've written, often between moms and kids, where I find myself sobbing at the keyboard. I know the characters better than I know anyone else, so it stands to reason that I'm emotionally invested in them.

Physically, when I write, I feel the years. I've been a writer for two decades and like every other writer I know, I have tendinitis. A good day writing can mean a very bad day for my arm or shoulder. I remind myself it's a pretty sweet problem to have.

Remember me?

I graduated from Princeton with a degree in creative writing/ English. A lot of my classmates and I got feeler letters from literary agents at big agencies: William Morris, CAA. I sent out my creative thesis—a novel you should be thrilled to know you'll never have to read—and didn't get any bites.

Since I'd never met anyone who was actually making a career out of writing, I had a backup plan. When I graduated from Princeton I had a job on Wall Street, writing bond-offering circulars for S&P and Moody's. I *hated* it. Hated it! I worked ninety hours a week, and at one point I figured out that I'd written more than a thousand pages about the company that makes Fiats.

When the stock market crashed in October 1987 I was delighted. I knew I'd be laid off, and I was. I used my severance package to buy a car and I moved to Massachusetts, where my boyfriend was living, and I got a job as a textbook editor.

Every day I'd finish my work by ten in the morning. Then I'd close the door to my office and pretend to be really busy. Actually, I was writing my second novel. Over the next two years, I worked as a textbook editor, as a teacher of creative writing at a private school, as an advertising copywriter. I got an M.Ed. at Harvard. I taught eighth grade English at a public school, and I got married and pregnant.

During that time, I kept pitching my novel to agents one at a time, picking their names out of *Literary Marketplace.* They all rejected me, some quite eloquently. Finally, one woman said yes. She was just starting her own agency. She'd never represented anyone, but thought she could represent me. I said yes, and she sold my first book in three months. That was twenty years ago, and she's still my agent.

After my books began to hit the *New York Times* list, I got a call from a bigwig New York literary agent. She wanted to fly me to New York to talk about representing me. I declined politely and said I had no intent of leaving my agent. I'm quite sure that this bigwig had no recollection that she'd been the very first agent to reject me.

Although I was published by age twenty-three, I wasn't making nearly enough money to support myself, let alone my family. My readership grew very slowly. I wasn't an overnight success—far from it. I didn't become a breadwinner until about 2004, when the paperback version of *My Sister's Keeper* sold enough copies that people began to recognize my name.

Home Depot time

My hardest time as a writer was when I realized that I'd grabbed the brass ring. I'd published a bunch of books, and I still wasn't a success.

A lot of writers think of the publishing contract as the Holy Grail, but it's not. It's a huge mistake to think that just because your book is being printed, your publisher will publicize it. If you're a new author, it's much more likely that they won't. You have to stump yourself and find book clubs to talk to and go to book fairs and set up signings at bookstores and libraries— anything to get word of mouth going. Your publisher's more likely to pay attention to your book if it starts magically selling. *Then* they might put some money into promoting it. It's a vicious cycle.

That's why I was really disheartened when I was a young mom of three kids, and I'd had multiple books published, but I was still toying with the idea of getting a job application from Home Depot so I could help support my family.

A movie deal isn't always what it's cracked up to be

Another really stressful time was during the filming of the movie that was made of my book *My Sister's Keeper*.

I'd explained to the production company how critical the ending of that book was. I'd gotten letters from readers saying that the ending was the reason they'd flung the book at their friends, saying, "Just read it so we can discuss it." The production company asked me to speak to the director they planned to hire before he signed on. I explained my concerns. He told me, "Yes, that's the right ending for this story. I won't change it, but if I have to for any reason, I'll tell you why and I'll tell you myself."

For two years, I helped him flesh out a script that was very close to the book. Then one day I got an e-mail from a fan who worked at a casting agency, telling me she had the script, and did I know the ending had changed?

To this day that director has never explained why he changed the end of the story, but because he did, the movie isn't anywhere near as powerful as the book. Apparently moviegoers agreed with me; the film wasn't a success at the box office.

The upside is that, as a result of that experience, I make sure I'm always offered creative control over my movie/television deals. That negative experience proved to me, and to people in the industry, that I know what I'm talking about.

Can't beat number one

The best time I've had as a writer is every time I've found out that a book of mine is debuting at number one on the *New York Times* bestseller list. It's happened a few times, and it never gets old. I have to pinch myself to say, Wow, look how far I've come. When I'm number one, I know it's not just my mom and her friends buying the book. I can remember the precise moment when my editor called with the good news. I'd write even if no one ever read my stuff, but it's so gratifying to know that people do.

Another amazing moment was when I did an event at the Margaret Mitchell House in Atlanta. *Gone with the Wind* is the book that made me want to be a writer. To sit at the desk where it was written had me trembling.

Surprise!

I know a lot of writers listen to music while they write, but I absolutely, positively cannot. Music is like Kryptonite to my writing.

It might also surprise you to know that I personally answer every single e-mail I get. I don't have an assistant, and I receive more than two hundred letters a day.

Jodi Picoult's Wisdom for Writers

- Take a writing course. It's how you'll learn to get and give feedback, and it'll teach you to write on demand.

- There's no magic bullet that'll make you a success. If you write because you want to be rich, you're in the wrong business. Write because you can't not write, or don't write at all.

- Write even when you don't feel like writing. There is no muse. It's hard work. You can always edit a bad page, but you can't edit a blank page.

- Read. It'll inspire you to write as well as the authors who came before you.

CHAPTER NINETEEN

Jane Smiley

He put his arm around her, squeezed hard. He knew, of course, that she adored him, or admired him, or whatever it was. He was one of those sorts of men that women were wiser to stay away from, men who took an interest in women, and observed them, and knew what they were thinking.

Darling, I should have been a different person. But I'm not.

—Page 16, Prologue, *Private Life*, 2010

Since her first book was published in 1980, Jane Smiley has written eleven novels, five nonfiction books, and three young adult novels.

We're talking Pulitzer Prize–winning, Lifetime Achievement Award–earning works of fiction and nonfiction, with topics as various as nineteenth-century farm life, an uncelebrated computer inventor, and the urban real estate boom of the 1980s. Smiley's running start on a writing career was cultivated by four years at Vassar, followed by a Fulbright Fellowship—in Iceland; where else would she have gone to study the medieval literature known as the Icelandic sagas?—and a stint at the vaunted Iowa Writers' Workshop.

Jane Smiley is a scholar as well as a writer and lover of the novel. She returned to Iowa to teach in the MFA program from which she graduated, and she has judged many a literary contest, including the 2009 Man Booker International Prize. Unlike many other great intellects, Jane Smiley likes to share, as evidenced by her exuberant 2005 study, *Thirteen Ways of Looking at the Novel*. "If to live is to progress," she wrote, "if you are lucky, from foolishness to wisdom, then to write novels is to broadcast the various stages of your foolishness."

Fans struggle through the time between Smiley's broadcasts, awaiting her next "foolishness" with great anticipation.

THE VITALS

Birthday: September 26, 1949

Born and raised: Born in Los Angeles, California; raised in Webster Groves, Missouri

Current home: Rural Northern California

Love life: Lives with Jack Canning; they won't say if they're legally married

Family life: Daughter Phoebe born 1978; daughter Lucy born 1982; son, Axel, born 1992

Schooling: BA, Vassar; MFA and PhD, University of Iowa

Teaching: Iowa State, undergrad and graduate creative writing workshops, 1981–96

Day job?: No

Honors and awards (partial listing): Pulitzer Prize, 1992; inducted into American Academy of Arts and Letters, 2001; PEN Center USA Lifetime Achievement Award for Literature, 2006; chaired judging panel for Man Booker International Prize, 2009

Notable notes:

- In 1992 Jane Smiley won the Pulitzer Prize for her fifth novel, *A Thousand Acres*.
- Smiley boards horses at a ranch near her home and rides nearly every day.
- Smiley writes and blogs for a wide range of magazines including the *New Yorker*, *Elle*, *Harper's*, *Playboy*, and *Practical Horseman*.

THE COLLECTED WORKS

<u>Novels</u>

Barn Blind, 1980

At Paradise Gate, 1981

Duplicate Keys, 1984

The Greenlanders, 1988

A Thousand Acres, 1991

Moo, 1995

The All-True Travels and Adventures of Lidie Newton, 1998

Horse Heaven, 2000

Good Faith, 2003

Ten Days in the Hills, 2007

Private Life, 2010

<u>Young Adult Novels</u>

The Georges and the Jewels, 2009

A Good Horse, 2010

True Blue, 2011

Jane Smiley

Why I write

I write to investigate things I'm curious about.

A novelist's job is to integrate information with the feelings and the stories of her characters, because a novel is about the alternation of the inner world and the outer world, what happens and what the characters feel about it. There's no reason to write a novel unless you're going to talk about the inner lives of your characters. Without that, the material is dry. But without events and information, the novel seems subjective and pointless.

You can see in the earliest novels, as they were forming themselves historically, that there was this impulse to find out stuff. Don Quixote thinks he's setting out to save something, but what he's really doing, as Cervantes follows him along, is finding out how the world works in comparison to how he thought it worked from reading his beloved romances. The whole point of *Don Quixote* is to show the conflict between what he thought was true and what he learns when he goes out there. It's not only a seminal work, it's the seminal motive for writing a novel.

When I was researching the nonfiction book I wrote about the novel, I discovered the childhoods of most novelists were similar to mine. Almost all novelists grew up reading voraciously, and many of them come from families in which it's automatic to tell stories about family characters, Aunt Ruth or whomever, and they are curious and/or observant. I was one of those kids who had to be told to stop asking questions all the time. That's what novelists do. We gather information, and we form what we learn into a story.

I loved to read, and I read lots of series books, such as Nancy Drew and the Bobbsey twins. I considered the novelists I read to be my friends. I wasn't intimidated by them—they were doing me a favor, telling me these stories. When I got older, in high school, I discovered that the American writer-ideal was Hemingway for a boy or Fitzgerald for a girl. An aspiring author of serious literature could be a he-man writer like Hemingway or a she-man writer like Fitzgerald. There were no female-writer role models.

Imagine a girl sitting at her desk in ninth grade, scratching her head, saying, I can't write *The Sun Also Rises*; I'm a girl. My only alternative is *The Great Gatsby*. But look what happened to Fitzgerald: he published four books and died of alcoholism and his first book was the only good one. Who wants *that*?

In college I found my other options: Virginia Woolf, Brontë,

Austen. But they weren't Americans. So I got used to looking to England for role models.

A pebble becomes a seed

When I'm in the act of writing, more than any other emotion, I feel *excited*.

I can't say I'm never frustrated, but I've been at this a really long time now, so I have ways of dealing with the frustration. I know that at some point in every day's writing, there will be a sort of takeoff. It might be early, it might be late, but there's a place where I feel the energy moving *itself* forward, instead of me pushing it.

One of the things I like about writing is that sense of the story unfolding. You throw this pebble into your story because you can't think of anything better, just to keep going. Then it stops being a little pebble and starts being a little seed, and suddenly it has shoots. It begins to grow.

I'm writing a book now that I'm sure will see the light of day, but God knows when. It's a what-if book about one of my horses: what if she were racing at Auteuil, the jumper course outside Paris? And what if she got out of her stall and headed into Paris? It's a really fun idea, but it has high levels of plausibility problems.

While I was working on it the other day, I came to a bump in the road. I didn't know *what* to do next. So I introduced a raven. He started out as a pebble. Then I looked up some facts about ravens, and then those were pretty interesting. I could feel the shoots begin around the raven. I could feel him start to speak in his own voice, becoming a little self-important, and suddenly the energy of the narrative entered into his voice. He became a raven from a long noble family of ravens, very proud of himself, very talkative. Somehow in the next few weeks he's going to help the horse.

That's what I like the most about writing a story: the way a *thing* comes in as a pebble and blossoms.

How I knew

During my senior year at Vassar, I wrote a novel as my senior thesis. It was an adolescent novel about the traumatic relationship of two college students. It's somewhere in the Vassar library now.

Knowing that I was going to be a writer was a function of knowing that I really enjoyed writing that novel. It grew out of curiosity—and the other thing that all my work (and a lot of literary work) grows out of, which is gossip. There was a girl and a guy in my class, and even though they weren't connected, I brought them together because they were the two weirdest people I knew. I can barely remember that novel now, but I remember how much I enjoyed writing it. It was much, much fun, and *that* was *that* for me.

My own private Iowa

In 1975, the year after I graduated from Vassar, I applied to the Iowa Writers' Workshop. I was rejected, but my husband was accepted to the history department, so we moved to Iowa. I worked in a teddy bear factory. Someone else stuffed the teddy bears. My job was to sew the back seam.

The next year I applied to the workshop again. This time I got in. My fellow students were quite good. We had Allan Gurganus, Jayne Anne Phillips, T. C. Boyle, John Givens, Richard Bausch. Everyone was very dedicated and professional and kind. Then I got a Fulbright and went to Iceland for a year. I'd spent most of grad school studying Old Icelandic literature, and I was going to write my PhD dissertation about it. My adviser said, "We don't really need another dissertation on Old Icelandic. We have enough of those already." So I turned in stories I had written instead, and then after I graduated, I wrote the first part of my first real novel.

The best of times

Writing my third novel was the best time I've ever had as a writer. I felt I was being manipulated from afar.

It seemed that the characters were using me as a secretary to write their story. I really enjoyed that. Every day I'd go sit in front of the typewriter and I'd join my characters in fourteenth-century Greenland, Europe's most far-flung trading outpost, and I'd put on my imaginary bearskin coat, and it would all just come out.

About twelve years later, I had a similar experience with another novel. That one also felt like I was being told the story, this time by the horse out in the barn, Mr. T.

The other books weren't bad experiences. Just different.

It gets better . . .

I believe that you either love the work or the rewards. Life is a lot easier if you love the work.

I'm lucky. I like the work more all the time. I'm even more curious now. I have more ideas. I'm more enthusiastic. I have more faith that the pebble will turn into a seed. My great fear is not that I'll run out of subjects. It's that I'll run out of time.

If you're curious, there's always a subject to write about. I always was interested in the outer world. I'll paste in a few things from my inner life if there's nothing else to put in, but it's not my goal in life to write about myself.

Some of my books have been more carefully planned than others. When I was writing *A Thousand Acres*, based on Shakespeare's *King Lear*, I made a rule that I couldn't diverge from Shakespeare's plot. That got sticky. For example: No, they couldn't have a war! They were a farm family in Iowa. So I gave them a legal battle instead.

When I was about two-thirds of the way through, I realized that I *had* departed from the plot. I had to go back and fix it. If a book has a plan, it's more difficult to write than a book that just has a form.

Ten Days in the Hills had a form rather than a plan. I knew it was going to be ten days. I knew that each of the days was going to be about equal in length. I really wanted the book to be 444 pages long. I don't know why; it just came to me as a kind of puzzle. I thought the structure of the puzzle would compensate for the looseness of the quote-unquote plot.

As I saw the word count mount up, I thought, Hmm, we could have real numbers here. I have to say, my editor wasn't sympathetic to the number magic. She got a little irritated with my desire to make *Ten Days* exactly 444 pages long.

Except when it gets worse

I wrote one of my novels in first person, and it was dead on arrival—I think because my protagonist wasn't the sort of person who'd know or say the things that needed to be said.

So I switched to third person and rewrote it. In that draft there was too much information. My protagonist's inner voice had disappeared. The characters kept lying there, semidead. Even though I was fearful and anxious, I couldn't stop going back to it. I thought it was a story worth telling.

The turning point came at draft four or five. I asked my accountant's book group to read it. They really liked it, and they also had appropriate suggestions. That was the moment I knew the book wasn't a lost cause, because it appealed to its audience, mature women.

I've never given up on a novel. Although I had my doubts about *A Thousand Acres*. I was writing it in the winter in this little office in our new house in Ames, Iowa. I kept falling asleep as I wrote. I put the manuscript aside, thinking it must be really boring. Then spring came and I reread it, and it seemed pretty good.

It turned out the chimney of the furnace was leaking carbon monoxide. When we stopped using the furnace, the novel stopped putting me to sleep. The lesson there is, sometimes it's not as bad as you think.

Rumors of the novel's death have been greatly exaggerated

The novel as a form is extremely capacious. They've been saying the novel is dying forever and ever, and it's still here. Of course I'm worried about the future of the novel. But I'm not *worried* about it. The novel is irreplaceable.

Or not

In the 1980s, publishing companies began to consolidate, and they got bigger and bigger. In the '90s, everyone rode the gravy train. Then the train crashed.

For writers, there's always been a tension between money and fame. If you're on the money side, that's your compensation. You can do what Jodi Picoult talked about in terms of being labeled "chick lit" versus "literary fiction": "weep into her check." If you're on the fame side, and your books are too complex to be bestsellers, that's your compensation.

Now advances are getting smaller. Bookstores are going under. Who knows what's going to happen? The real question is, how big a hit will the audience take? Kids are reading books; that's the only good sign there is. That doesn't mean it's going to pan out, but it's something.

What we have to look at in the death of the novel is the departure of male readers. The lionization of Updike and Mailer and those guys depended on the male infrastructure of literature: editors, reviewers, kvellers picking the dominant male; writers arguing among themselves about who was the dominant male. That culture of male dominance is gone now. They keep trying to revive it with Jonathan Franzen, but unless men come back to reading, it's not going to revive.

I say, let's talk about Franzen after his tenth book. Let's see if there's consistency in his body of work.

Boys and girls—together?

If you ask a group of men how many books by women they've read in the past year, no hands will go up. If you ask a group of women how many books by men or women they've read, it's about equal. I'm one of them. I read both.

In 2005 the *New York Times Book Review* asked me to blog about a survey they did. They asked two hundred editors, authors, and critics—one hundred men, one hundred women—to name the best books of the past forty years. *Beloved* came in first. The next ten books were by men. Then came Marilynne Robinson.

Men returned sixty-two percent of the surveys that came back. Except for *Beloved*, they all voted for male writers. The women voted for both women and men. A lot of women didn't bother to vote. I wrote in my blog that maybe the women didn't believe in that hierarchical view of literature. They thought it was a stupid question, whereas the men thought it was an important question.

Curiouser and curiouser

Believe me, I'm not complaining. I've been really lucky. It does still happen that I go to my publisher and say, "I have this idea," and they say, *"What?"* When I went to my agent with *A Thou-*

sand Acres, she said, "Are you kidding? Nobody wants to read about *crops*." Then I turned in the book, and it was fine.

I've had some rewards. Rewards are fantasies. You can't wish for an award. You cannot say, "My career will finally be worth it if I win the Nobel Prize." That's false consciousness.

If your career wasn't worth it while you were writing those books, then what a sad life you've led. For me, it goes back to curiosity. I suppose my career will be over when I look around and say, "This is all boring; there's nothing more that interests me."

You want your interests to outrun your actual days on earth.

Jane Smiley's Wisdom for Writers

- Don't write a book you think a publisher will want to publish. Write the book you want to research and the book you want to read.

- When you're a novelist, you're a gossiper of the imaginary. You can take people you know who don't know each other and make them fall in love. The fun part is seeing what happens.

- Figure out who your readership is for whatever you're writing, and try it out on a group of those people—or a book group whose members are that kind of person.

CHAPTER TWENTY

Meg Wolitzer

People like to warn you that by the time you reach the middle of your life, passion will begin to feel like a meal eaten long ago, which you remember with great tenderness. The bright points of silver. The butter in its oblong dish. The corpse of a chocolate cake. The leaning back in a chair at the end, slugged on the head and overcome. . . .

—Opening lines, *The Uncoupling*, 2011

"Meg Wolitzer," Nick Hornby wrote in the *Believer*, "is an author who makes you wonder why more people don't write perceptive, entertaining, unassuming novels about how and why ordinary people choose to make decisions about their lives."

Hornby's praise is understated, verging on dismissive. Perceptive and entertaining, yes, but unassuming? Not so much. Meg Wolitzer's wit and popularity should not be cause to mistake her for a literary lite. Wolitzer starts small and goes wide, and her mission is ambitious: to depict who we average Americans really are, when no one's looking.

Wolitzer took a distinctly *assuming* position on the subject in the *New York Times Book Review* on March 30, 2012, writing in essay form what every one of her novels demands. "Many first-rate books by women and about women's lives never find a way to escape 'Women's Fiction,'" she wrote, "and make the leap onto the upper shelf where certain books, most of them written by men, . . . are prominently displayed and admired."

THE VITALS

Birthday: May 28, 1959

Born and raised: Born in Brooklyn; grew up on Long Island, New York

Current home: Manhattan

Love life: Married to science writer Richard Panek

Kids: Gabriel, born 1990; Charlie, born 1995

Schooling: Studied creative writing at Smith College; graduated from Brown University, 1981

Day job?: No

Honors and awards (partial listing): National Endowment for the Arts grant, 1994; included in *Best American Short Stories*, 1998; Pushcart Prize, 1998

Notable notes:

- Meg Wolitzer is a self-described Scrabble nerd who prefers playing anonymously online. Hence the protagonist of her recent young adult novel, a boy who possesses magic powers that allow him to win at Scrabble.
- After reading Wolitzer's latest novel, *The Uncoupling*, Suzzy Roche of the Roches liked it so much she wrote a song based on it, "Back in the Sack."
- Meg Wolitzer's mother is novelist Hilma Wolitzer.

Website: www.megwolitzer.com

Facebook: www.facebook.com/megwolitzerauthor

Twitter: @MegWolitzer

THE COLLECTED WORKS

Novels

Sleepwalking, 1982

Hidden Pictures, 1986

This Is Your Life, 1988

Friends for Life, 1994

Surrender, Dorothy, 1998

The Wife, 2003

The Position, 2005

The Ten-Year Nap, 2008

The Uncoupling, 2011

Film and TV Adaptations

This Is My Life (based on *This Is Your Life*), 1992

Surrender, Dorothy, 2006

Young Adult Novel

The Fingertips of Duncan Dorfman, 2011

Meg Wolitzer

Why I write

Though it's pleasing, as a writer, to think that most of your life is a quest toward doing the kind of work that absorbs you most, sometimes I think that a good deal of my life is, perhaps, essentially a quest toward freedom from anxiety. Being engaged in prose, especially when it's going well, can keep the anxiety of the world away.

Writing is the only thing I know that can do that; the work becomes an airtight container. Poisonous things are not allowed in; after all, you're the bouncer! You have deep control, and where else can you find that? You can't control other people or your relationships or your children, but in writing you can have sustained periods where you're absolutely in charge.

I write, as Zadie Smith said, to reveal my way of being in the world, my sensibility. What am I but my sensibility: my self, my experiences, the changes I've made and seen?

A certain kind of writer writes to meet her ghosts. I'm not brave in that way. In a sense I need to be *lanced* when I write. Nor do I write or read to escape. There is no escape; I don't know what that even means. When I work, I want to achieve a sort of tilt, to create a skewed world, an interesting world.

I like the physical sensation of writing, too. It gives me a kind of ruddy vigor, like some sort of exercise you want a reward for afterward. I find it deeply satisfying to have worked something out in a novel. My husband's a science writer, and this is the closest I'm ever going to get to his world, to working on cosmic puzzles and theories.

I'm a big Scrabble player, and I used to write puzzles. With my cowriter Jesse Green, I created a weekly cryptic crossword for *7 Days* magazine in New York, way back when. Sometimes I think of writing as being like that: cryptic, filled with clues, inscrutable, elegant. What's the way out of the locked room of the hell of a novel going nowhere? I've been known to jump up and down (well, subtly) when I come up with a solution to a problem in my fiction. Working it out is a kind of exercise you've given yourself that no one else will give you. It's a very personalized form of homework.

I write to hammer out an idea that I'd be hammering out in my head anyway—to make some kind out concrete thing out of it. It's a natural extension of the inner jabber. When I have inner jabber plus imperative, that's a book.

Writing for Mom

I had a fairly unusual situation, growing up: I had a mother who was a writer, though unlike me, she came to writing very late. I was six or seven when she sold her first short story to the old *Saturday Evening Post*. I saw the pain and excitement of her experiences. When I started writing, I wrote for her.

In first grade, I had a teacher who'd invite me up to her desk, and I'd dictate stories to her, because she could write them down faster than I could. My mother saved the stories, and looking at them now, I can see that I started to write as a way of figuring out the world. As I got a little older, I loved to rush home and show my mother what I'd written, knowing there would be an encouraging response.

I gave a reading once, and an older woman stood up and said that her daughter was trying to be a playwright, and she was worried that her daughter wouldn't be able to make a living. I said she should encourage her talents, and that the world would do its best to whittle away at her daughter, but a mother should never do that.

At Brown, I studied with the great writer John Hawkes, who we all called Jack. One day I ran into him on campus, and because I wanted to please him, a lie sprang to my lips. I blurted out, "I just finished writing a story." Then I had to run home and actually write it.

Later on in a writing life, when you're being published fairly frequently and you don't have to obsessively please another person, there's no thrilling Helen Keller "water" moment, but a series of moments: the excitement of knowing that you're not writing into the void, that here's a vessel for your work. That protégé/mentor thing is a way in, and then eventually you don't need it anymore.

Shame

I sold my first novel to Random House for five thousand dollars while I was still at Brown. It came out eighteen months later.

I was all set to go to Stanford for grad school, but I decided to move to New York City and see if I could make it as a writer instead. I lived in the Village and ate tons of Indian takeout. I wasn't focused on money. All I knew was, I'd sold my novel and I wanted to live as a fiction writer.

I went to MacDowell [Colony] right after I moved to New York. It was so long ago that I had my folk guitar with me, with its no-nukes sticker on the side, and I sat under a tree and played "The Water Is Wide." Do I distance myself from that girl? Absolutely not. Living with our own ridiculousness is something writers have to do.

Over the next few years I kept selling novels for incrementally slightly larger advances. It was such a different era, and it never occurred to me to think of how many—or how few—copies I was selling. I felt I was successful simply because I was being published. I was very grateful and happy. It never occurred to me that this joy could be in peril, but of course it always is. Some of the writers I came up with eventually disappeared. Was it because they couldn't get published anymore? Because they just stopped writing? In some cases I really don't know.

I never had any money until 1992, when one of my books was made into a movie. It was perfect timing. I had a new baby, and I had no idea how I was going to write and also be a parent. The movie deal bought me time. It got me off the hamster wheel of writing and teaching.

I've resumed my place on that hamster wheel now, because I have a kid in college, and one who's rapidly heading there. As I've mentioned, my husband's a writer, too, so we're both living that fragile, one-foot-on-a-banana-peel life. We make corrections as we need to. I feel that there's no shame in doing whatever you need to do to make a living as a writer. It's exhausting but exciting.

I was in a car full of writers once, being driven to some event, and everyone in the backseat was talking about our failures and disappointments. The driver turned around and burst out, "You're all so talented! Why should you feel so much shame?" We had to laugh at ourselves. We knew we were describing a feeling that a lot of writers have.

Sometimes Zeus. Sometimes not.

I have very different kinds of writing days. With some books, I have that springing-from-the forehead-of-Zeus, improbable, and productive experience. There might be day after day of engagement, and the world drops away, the contents of my brain recast in miniature on the page. When I was writing my novel *The Position*, I had the feeling that I was simply the amanuensis.

It was my job to write the book down like a secretary. I wrote that book very fast.

With other books, there might be days and days of fatigue and lethargy—and in my own experience, this ends up being because there's a faulty or not fully realized imperative at the heart of the book.

The imperative: imperative

While I'm writing, I ask myself the question that a reader inevitably asks a writer: why are you telling me this? There has to be an erotic itch, a sense of book as hot object, the idea that what's contained in the book is the information you've always needed.

If the answer to the question "Why are you telling me this?" doesn't come quickly, if I'm writing without urgency, that's my first sign that something's amiss. When novels or stories feel like they're going nowhere, they've lost their imperative, their reason for being.

Imperative is the kind of thing we associate with urgent, external moments—say, with political causes. I also associate it with art. You know that something might be righted, whether it's a social wrong or incomplete information. That's what art gives you: a more complete view, a view of corners you wouldn't otherwise have seen.

Years ago, I sold a novel based on Freud's famous patient Dora, written from her point of view, essentially attempting to reclaim her story from Freud and return it to her. I really enjoyed writing the first fifty pages, and I traveled to Vienna to research it. And then, not long afterward, I realized that I didn't want to write this book. I felt constrained by the language I had to use because it was set in a long-ago time, and it was a first-person book. Reclaiming the narrative and returning it to her was great in theory but not in reality. Once I knew that, I lost the imperative to write it.

Some novels are like big pocketbooks; they've got the whole world in them, and the writer and the reader have to dig around a bit to find what they're looking for. Some novels are more slender containers. This one would have had to be the latter kind. I was surprised I had so much trouble, because I'm very interested in psychoanalysis, and I thought such a book would be a way to write about the subject with force. But I found myself relying too heavily on lyricism, which, for me, is something of a trap.

Lyricism can break sentences into shining, separate, discrete objects, and that can either contribute to a work's power or merely make the prose feel pretty, writerly, and admirable, but lacking in force. My trip to Vienna ended up as a single paragraph in my next novel after I dropped Dora and her world. Everything makes a good soup eventually, even if in a totally unrecognizable form.

The most difficult time for me as a writer is before I have a central guiding idea for a book. Once I have it I feel reassured. It's like having an inhaler in your pocket, if you're an asthmatic.

Before and after

I divide my writing life into periods of before and after I wrote *The Wife*. I don't like much of what I'd written before that book. I was still living in a world of sentences that were sometimes pleasing to me, but I wasn't happy with them. I was keeping myself self-consciously lyrical and held-back and a little reserved as a writer. I worried that the results weren't forceful enough.

The stuff I liked to read at the time was so much stronger than what I was actually writing. While I have some reservations about Philip Roth's work, I love the muscularity of it. What was keeping me from writing with the kind of fervor I felt when I was reading? I took that on directly when I wrote *The Wife*.

Rock, paper, scissors

I'd conceived *The Uncoupling* as a contemporary *Lysistrata*. I started it during the Bush years, when, like everyone else, I was fatigued by the endless wars the United States had started in Afghanistan and Iraq. Initially, I thought *The Uncoupling* would have a significant war content.

Then there was a shift as I wrote. I always know, when I dutifully return to a balky, "stuck" scene and realize that it won't be any reader's favorite, that it probably shouldn't be in the book. I started seeing scenes like that in *The Uncoupling*. And then what I knew I actually wanted to write about just rose up and overpowered the rest. It was a kind of rock-paper-scissors game in my mind. What interested me most in the *Lysistrata* story, finally, as a writer, wasn't the women using their sexual power to stop a war, but the way the play could allow me to take a look at sexual desire, and sexual fatigue in a marriage. It could allow me to look at female sexuality over time. So I reimagined the whole book.

Gratitude

These are not contemplative times, and writing is a contemplative experience. The idea that something is thoughtful and slow, and takes its time to reveal itself, is not in keeping with today's velocity.

I envy people who have more financial security, because the pressures of making a living will bear down on you. I know how lucky I am that I've managed to stay around as a writer. I never take that for granted.

Meg Wolitzer's Wisdom for Writers

- Writing that is effective is like a concentrate, a bouillon cube. You're not just choosing a random day and writing about that. You pick ordinary moments and magnify them—as if they're freeze-dried, so the reader can add water.

- To find the idea that guides your book, you might write freely for a couple of chapters. Then take a look at what you've made, and you'll start to understand what the fabric of it is. Then go on and write, say, eighty pages of it. Not a hundred; if you get to one hundred and end up putting it aside, you might feel like you wasted so much time. I sometimes recommend writing around eighty pages, which is a solid mass of pages and something to feel proud of. Then look over it and begin to map out where the book is going.

- I always ask for the wisdom of writer friends whom I trust, and I always listen very closely to what they have to say. Be sure to pick a trustworthy "designated reader."

- No one can take writing away from you, but no one can give it to you, either.

The author will donate a portion of her royalties from *Why We Write* to 826 National.

826 National is a nonprofit organization that ensures the success of its network of eight writing and tutoring centers, which each year assist nearly 30,000 young people. Its mission is based on the understanding that great leaps in learning can happen with one-on-one attention, and that strong writing skills are fundamental to future success.

826 centers offer a variety of inventive workshops and publishing programs that provide under-resourced students, ages 6–18, with opportunities to explore their creativity and improve their writing skills. They also aim to help teachers get their classes excited about writing.

For more information or to make a donation, visit the website www.826national.org.